Why Reading Comp

The key to reading is understanding wh___ child can become a better reader, but ___ ___ not necessarily improve his or her reading comprehension. The ability to comprehend what is read is critical to understanding textbooks in later grades, which is why you will find this book has a majority of nonfiction passages. The book repeats important strategies necessary for strengthening reading comprehension skills. By completing the book in order, your child will revisit the strategies.

Upon your child's completion of each activity, use the provided incentive chart and stickers to track progress and celebrate your child's success.

SKILLS

- Author's purpose
- Cause and effect
- Fact vs. opinion
- Nonfiction features
- Sequencing
- Using context clues
- Identifying character traits
- Identifying main ideas and details

STRATEGIES

- Questioning
- Using background knowledge
- Making connections
- Determining importance
- Rereading

HOW YOU CAN HELP SUPPORT LEARNING

- Encourage your child to read every day and use the *What Genre Am I Reading?* recording sheet on page 2 to keep track of the books he or she reads each month.
- Create a clear space, free of distractions, for your child to read and answer the questions.
- Remind your child to read each passage at least twice before answering the questions.
- As your child reads a passage, ask questions related to the text. Ask about the characters or people and the passage's theme. Discuss the main ideas and details.
- Have your child summarize each passage before answering the questions.
- Ask your child, "What did you do that helped you understand this passage?"
- After answering the questions, help your child use the answer key to check his or her work.
- Work with your child to locate the correct answers for any incorrect responses.

Reprinted 2014
© 2012 Creative Teaching Press Inc., Huntington Beach, CA 92649
Reproduction of activities in any manner for use in the classroom and not for commercial sale is permissible.
Reproduction of these materials for an entire school or for a school system is strictly prohibited.

What Genre Am I Reading?

Record the genre for each book you read within the next month by coloring that section of the bar graph.

Genres I Read in the Month of _____

autobiography | biography | fantasy | historical fiction | informational text | mystery | poetry | realistic fiction | science fiction

Which genre did you read most often? _____

Which genre did you read least often? _____

Which genre is your favorite? _____

Name That Genre

Read each definition. Then fill in the bubble beside the correct answer.

1. A suspenseful story about a puzzling event that involves gathering clues or evidence to a solution, which is usually revealed at the end.
    - a) historical fiction
    - b) science fiction
    - c) realistic fiction
    - d) mystery

2. A nonfiction text written about a person by another person.
    - a) historical fiction
    - b) biography
    - c) autobiography
    - d) science fiction

3. A fictional story that takes place during a particular time period in the past. It often involves a real setting with characters or events that include fictional elements.
    - a) historical fiction
    - b) fantasy
    - c) realistic fiction
    - d) mystery

4. A story of a person's life written by that person.
    - a) autobiography
    - b) biography
    - c) fantasy
    - d) realistic fiction

5. A story using imaginary characters with events that could happen in real life.
    - a) historical fiction
    - b) realistic fiction
    - c) science fiction
    - d) fantasy

6. A nonfiction text that provides facts about a topic.
    - a) realistic fiction
    - b) mystery
    - c) informational
    - d) science fiction

© 2012 CTP - 7236

Author's Purpose in a Genre

Read each description of a text. Write the genre.
Then circle the author's purpose.

1. A cookbook with 101 recipes for making cake pops

   genre: _____

   author's purpose: entertain   persuade   inform   describe

2. A five-paragraph essay, written by a third-grade student, explaining why people should recycle and not litter

   genre: _____

   author's purpose: entertain   persuade   inform   describe

3. A book about the president, written by the vice president

   genre: _____

   author's purpose: entertain   persuade   inform   describe

4. A story about robots from Mars taking over the school

   genre: _____

   author's purpose: entertain   persuade   inform   describe

5. A story involving three friends who find an old key in an antique box and try to find what it might open

   genre: _____

   author's purpose: entertain   persuade   inform   describe

6. A book written by Jane Goodall describing how she began her efforts to help the chimpanzees at Gombe Stream National Park

   genre: _____

   author's purpose: entertain   persuade   inform   describe

7. A list of reasons why a student should be able to switch seats in the class

   genre: _____

   author's purpose: entertain   persuade   inform   describe

Inside an Informational Book

Answer the following questions.

1. What is found in a Table of Contents?
    a. a list of definitions of words that appear in the book
    b. a list of the parts of a book in the order in which they appear
    c. a list of words in alphabetical order, and their page numbers
    d. a list of the pictures in a book

2. Why do nonfiction texts include words in bold print?
   _____

3. Where can you find the meaning of boldfaced words?
   _____

4. What is the purpose of the index?
   _____

5. What are the sentences, or words, near diagrams and pictures called?
    a. definitions
    b. captions
    c. illustrations
    d. rules

6. When reading a nonfiction book, what should be examined before reading any page?
    a. the graphic elements (captions, sidebars, maps, diagrams, graphics, or images)
    b. the length of the page
    c. the visual cues (titles, headings, bold print, bulleted lists)
    d. both a and c

7. Which strategy helps improve nonfiction comprehension?
    a. taking notes as you read
    b. highlight key words or ideas
    c. reread new information, terms, or ideas
    d. all of the above

© 2012 CTP - 7236

5

Double Match

Match the nonfiction texts in the first column to their descriptions in the center column. Then match the descriptions to the signal words in the third column.

Nonfiction Text	Description	Signal Words
description	lists items or events in numerical order or in order of a timeline	• first • next • then • last • finally
sequence	lists characteristics, features, or examples	• but • however • same as • although
comparison/ contrast	two or more events, ideas, or concepts are alike or different	• for example • such as • is like
cause/ effect	there is a problem and one or more solutions	• because • problem is • so that
problem/ solution	there are events that happen and reasons for those events	• reasons why • therefore • because • as a result

Fact or Opinion?

Read the sentences below. Write **F** for fact and **O** for opinion.

1 _____ Making an ice cave is hard work.

2 _____ A bicycle has two wheels.

3 _____ Elephants are the most interesting animals to study.

4 _____ Zookeepers have the best jobs.

5 _____ Wearing a helmet keeps a person safer on a motorcycle.

6 _____ Everyone should wear kneepads when learning to ride a bike.

7 _____ Earning an allowance is an important way for children to learn about money.

8 _____ Hurricanes are scary.

9 _____ Swimming is the best Olympic event.

10 _____ Fog is a thick cloud close to the surface of the earth.

More Fact and Opinion

Fill in the bubble beside the correct answer.

1 Which form of writing would most likely have more opinions than facts?
- ⓐ how-to article
- ⓑ letter to a friend
- ⓒ report
- ⓓ news story

2 Which form of writing would have only facts?
- ⓐ persuasive essay
- ⓑ letter to a friend
- ⓒ report
- ⓓ mystery

3 Which form of writing could have both facts and opinions?
- ⓐ persuasive essay
- ⓑ mystery
- ⓒ report
- ⓓ how-to article

4 Select the title of the magazine article that would likely have more facts than opinions.
- ⓐ "Reasons Why I Think Carrots are the Best Vegetable"
- ⓑ "Dancing Is Fun!"
- ⓒ "The Destruction of the Rain Forest"
- ⓓ "My Worst Vacation Ever"

Horses

Read the passage. Draw a line under the facts and circle the opinions in the passage. Then answer the questions.

Horses are the most important animals for humans. For years, they have been used to pull loads, plow fields, and fight in wars. Today, many people still rely on the strength of horses to carry supplies and people from one place to another. Horses are beautiful creatures to watch. People gather to watch professional horse races and horseback riding competitions. Anyone who has ever touched a horse has fallen in love with it. However, keeping a horse is a big responsibility. Horses need food, shelter, and proper exercise. Owning and caring for a horse is everyone's dream.

1. What are three purposes of horses long ago?

_____

_____

_____

2. What do horses need?

_____

_____

_____

3. How are horses used today?

_____

_____

_____

Microwave Ovens

Read the passage. Then read each statement below.
Write **F** if it is a fact and **O** if it is an opinion.

Is there a microwave in your home? Do you know why food gets warmer when placed in a microwave? Microwaves work by heating the water or fats within foods. This explains why dry foods such as rice and pasta will not cook in the microwave unless they are in some water. As with any kitchen appliance or tool, it is important to follow these safety tips:

1. Always use microwave-safe containers.
2. Use a potholder when removing items from a microwave.
3. Allow time for the food or drink to cool.
4. Only use a microwave with the help of an adult.

As long as a microwave is used safely, it can be a useful tool in the kitchen.

1. _____ A microwave is the best way to cook food if you are in a hurry.

2. _____ Following the safety rules is important.

3. _____ Microwaves should only be used with an adult.

4. _____ As long as you are careful, you should eat your food right out of the microwave.

5. _____ Every house needs a microwave to cook food faster.

6. _____ Dry foods won't cook in a microwave.

7. _____ Microwaves heat water or fats in food.

8. _____ Microwaves are not very useful.

How to Make Microwave S'mores

Read the recipe. Then answer the questions.

Ingredients:
- 2 graham cracker squares
- 1 chocolate bar divided into squares
- 1 large marshmallow

Directions:
1. Put 1 graham cracker square on a plate.
2. Put the desired amount of chocolate on the graham cracker.
3. Put the marshmallow on the chocolate.
4. Put the plate in the microwave.
5. Turn on the microwave for 15 seconds or until the marshmallow is puffy.
6. Carefully open the microwave, and wait for everything to cool.
7. Remove the plate and put the other graham cracker on top of the marshmallow.
8. Eat it!

1. What is the author's purpose for writing this recipe?

_____

2. What do you need to do right before putting the marshmallow on the graham cracker? _____

3. What do you need to do right before putting the graham cracker in the microwave? _____

4. Why do you think it is important to stop the microwave when the marshmallow gets puffy? _____

5. Why is Step 6 important? _____

_____

Making Inferences

Read the passage. Then write **yes** on the line if it could be an inference you could make by reading the passage. Write **no** if it could not.

> Keith opened his new kite, attached the string, and walked to the beach for some fun in the sun. He held his kite and began to run. Just before heading home, he said, "Wow! That was the highest I've ever gotten my kite to fly!"

1. _____ Keith lives near the beach.

2. _____ Keith used his own allowance money to buy the kite.

3. _____ Keith took kite lessons.

4. _____ It was a windy day.

5. _____ Keith has flown a kite before.

6. _____ Keith went to the beach with a friend.

7. _____ Keith probably enjoys flying kites.

8. _____ Keith's kite has a picture of a dragon on it

Dotty

Read the passage. Then answer the questions.

Joy had always wanted a pet she could hold, groom, and cuddle. Now if she could only convince her dad to let her have one. She knew exactly what she wanted, the cage she would build, and the litter she needed to potty train it. After reading all about the pet, she knew it could be litter box trained even though most people would never imagine that.

Finally, the day arrived! She had done her research and was ready for the responsibility of owning a pet. She couldn't believe it when her dad actually said, "Yes!" The moment she saw Spotty Dotty in the window of the pet shop, Joy knew she was meant to be her new pet. As Spotty Dotty wiggled her nose, moved her long ears, and hopped across her small cage, she seemed as if she was looking right at Joy.

1. What things did Joy want to do with her pet?

_____

2. How did she know her pet could be litter box trained if most people did not?

_____

3. Where will her pet live?

_____

4. What type of animal was Joy's new pet?

_____

5. Is Joy prepared for the responsibility of a new pet? Why?

_____

Unique Ways to Use Lemons

Read the passage and the statements that follow. Write **F** if it is a **fact** that was stated in the passage. Write **I** if it is an **inference** you had to make based on the facts and what you already know.

When you think of lemons, what is the first word that comes to mind? Can you picture the look on a person's face who tastes a lemon for the first time? Have you ever tasted a lemon? Perhaps you've tried selling lemonade to your friends and neighbors at a lemonade stand. Most people think of lemonade as the only purpose for a lemon, but that is not true. Lemons have been used for many other reasons. First, lemons are a safe and natural way to clean copper pans, tea stains off clothes, and cutting boards. A second use for lemons is in stopping apples from turning brown after they are cut. Simply squirt lemon juice on the apples after cutting. Third, lemons can be used to eliminate bad smells from kitchen drains. To do this, just toss some lemon slices into the sink's garbage disposal and turn it on. As you can see, lemons can be used in ways other than for making tasty lemonade!

1. _____ Lemons can be used in several different ways.

2. _____ Squirting lemon juice on apples before cutting them will keep them from turning brown.

3. _____ Lemons can be used for cleaning instead of chemicals.

4. _____ Lemons taste sour.

5. _____ Lemons eliminate bad smells.

6. List four uses for lemons on the lines below.

_____

_____

_____

_____

How to Make Lemonade

Read the recipe. Then answer the following questions.

Prep time: 10 minutes   **Yield:** 6 cups   **Difficulty level:** Easy

Ingredients:
- 1 cup sugar
- 1 cup water
- juice from 6 lemons
- 4 cups of cold water

Directions:
1. Heat the sugar and water in a pot until the sugar dissolves to make sugar water.
2. Squeeze the juice from 6 lemons into a pitcher.
3. Add the sugar water to the pitcher.
4. Add the cold water.
5. Cool for 30 to 40 minutes in the refrigerator.
6. Serve with ice.

1. What do you need to do first to make lemonade?
   a) squeeze the lemons
   b) take out the ice
   c) make sugar water

2. What do you do before adding the cold water?
   a) cool in the refrigerator
   b) add sugar water
   c) add ice

3. What do you do after squeezing the juice from the lemons?
   a) mix with sugar water
   b) cool for 30 to 40 minutes
   c) squeeze 6 lemons

4. What do you think would happen to the lemonade if you squeezed 12 lemons instead of 6?

   _____

5. How do you think the lemonade would be different if you used 3 cups of sugar instead of 1?

   _____

© 2012 CTP - 7236

Police Officers

Read the passage. Then read each statement below and fill in the bubble beside the answer that shows how the statement relates to the passage.

Have you ever thought about being a police officer some day? Perhaps you have seen one on the road or in a store. What exactly does a police officer do in a community? A police officer has many important roles related to enforcing the laws and keeping people safe. To be a police officer, a person needs to be healthy, honest, and have other good character traits.

1. A police officer needs to drive a car or motorcycle.
- ⓐ in the text
- ⓑ can be inferred from the text as true
- ⓒ can be inferred from the text as false
- ⓓ cannot be inferred from the text and needs further research

2. Being responsible and trustworthy are characteristics of police officers.
- ⓐ in the text
- ⓑ can be inferred from the text as true
- ⓒ can be inferred from the text as false
- ⓓ cannot be inferred from the text and needs further research

3. Police officers are community helpers who keep people safe.
- ⓐ in the text
- ⓑ can be inferred from the text as true
- ⓒ can be inferred from the text as false
- ⓓ cannot be inferred from the text and needs further research

4. Even if you eat junk food and never exercise, you can become a police officer.
- ⓐ in the text
- ⓑ can be inferred from the text as true
- ⓒ can be inferred from the text as false
- ⓓ cannot be inferred from the text and needs further research

Police Officers Wanted

Read the newspaper advertisement. Then answer the questions.

WANTED: UNDERCOVER POLICE OFFICER

The Yountville Police Department is seeking undercover police officers to help monitor suspicious behavior in stores and in the community. Complete the application form located on the police department's website, www.yountvillepolice.org. Include your experience in safety; why you want to be an undercover police officer; your current health; and your favorite hobbies.

Please submit applications no later than July 7 to: Inspector Olson, Yountville Police Department.

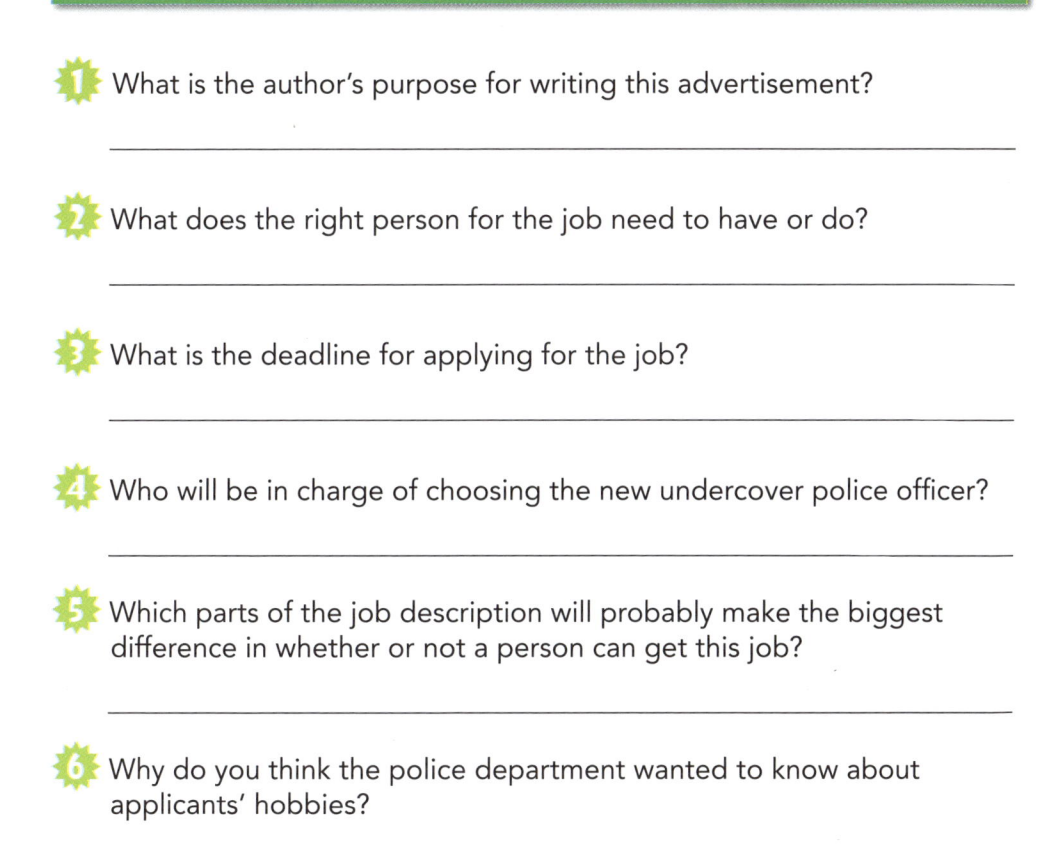

---

1. What is the author's purpose for writing this advertisement?
   _____

2. What does the right person for the job need to have or do?
   _____

3. What is the deadline for applying for the job?
   _____

4. Who will be in charge of choosing the new undercover police officer?
   _____

5. Which parts of the job description will probably make the biggest difference in whether or not a person can get this job?
   _____

6. Why do you think the police department wanted to know about applicants' hobbies?
   _____

Honey

Read the passage. Then answer the questions.

Do you know which is the only insect that produces food eaten by humans? That's right! It's the honeybee. Honey is the only food that includes all of the substances necessary to live, including vitamins, minerals, and water. Did you know that honey comes in different shades and flavors? Darker honeys have more nutrients than lighter ones. There are over 300 unique flavors of honey in the United States, including maple, raspberry, and blackberry. The most common honey found in stores is called clover honey. In addition to being used with food, honey can also be used for medicinal purposes. Honey can help people suffering from allergies, heal cuts, and soothe a sore throat. The next time you see honey, take a closer look!

1. Based on the context clues, what are the nutrients found in honey?
    a. flavors
    b. vitamins, minerals, and water
    c. darker and lighter
    d. maple, raspberry, and blackberry

2. Based on the context clues, what does it mean to "use honey for its medicinal purposes"?
    a. how it makes food taste better
    b. how honey makes medicine
    c. how honey can help people in ways similar to medicine
    d. how honey can be sold to buy medicine

3. If you see two bottles of honey, one with darker honey and one lighter in color, what will you know?
    a. the darker honey is rotten
    b. the darker honey is hotter
    c. the lighter honey is not as heavy
    d. the darker honey has more vitamins and minerals

4. Write a fact about honey.

_____

The Beekeeper's Day

Read the To-Do List and Daily Log. Then answer the questions.

To-Do List for Today:

- Check the hives for insects, birds, and other intruders.

- Watch spy cam for skunk visit last night.

- Collect honey from the hives.

Daily Log

1:00 Speak at the Beekeepers Association Lunch about bee behavior when visited at night by skunks. Warn them of signs such as aggressive behavior the next day.

2:30 Check the bee swarms at Zydez Farm.

4:00 Make honey ice cream for the birthday party.

5:00 Bee Club meeting. Discuss how to keep intruders out of the hives.

6:30 Beatrice's birthday party.

1 What dessert will be served at Beatrice's birthday party?
_____

2 Using context clues, do you think that insects and birds are good or bad for a beehive? Why or why not?
_____
_____

3 Using context clues, do you think that skunks are good or bad for a beehive? Why or why not?
_____
_____

4 Use a dictionary to find the meaning of *aggressive*. What would aggressive behavior in bees most likely include?
_____
_____

Welcome to My Backyard

Read the passage. Then answer the questions on page 21.

Have you ever heard someone use the saying, "Lay out the welcome mat?" It means to do something that invites someone or something. Did you know that there are things that can be added to a garden or around a home to welcome certain living things?

If you want to lay out the welcome mat for hummingbirds, then you should plant some red flowers. Would you enjoy seeing more butterflies in your backyard? If so, then you can add a flowering plant called *Buddleia*, or butterfly bush. Watch out! The butterfly bush will also attract bees. If you really want more bees in your yard, you could also plant some lavender. A bonus of planting lavender is that it will keep fleas and moths away. Perhaps you love watching or holding ladybugs. To attract more ladybugs, you might want to plant some yarrow. The leaves of the yarrow plant can also be made into a tea that can help with a stomachache.

If the idea of any of these creatures leaves you with a stomachache, then you now know which plants to keep out of your garden!

Welcome to My Backyard

Use the passage on page 20 to write the missing cause or effect.

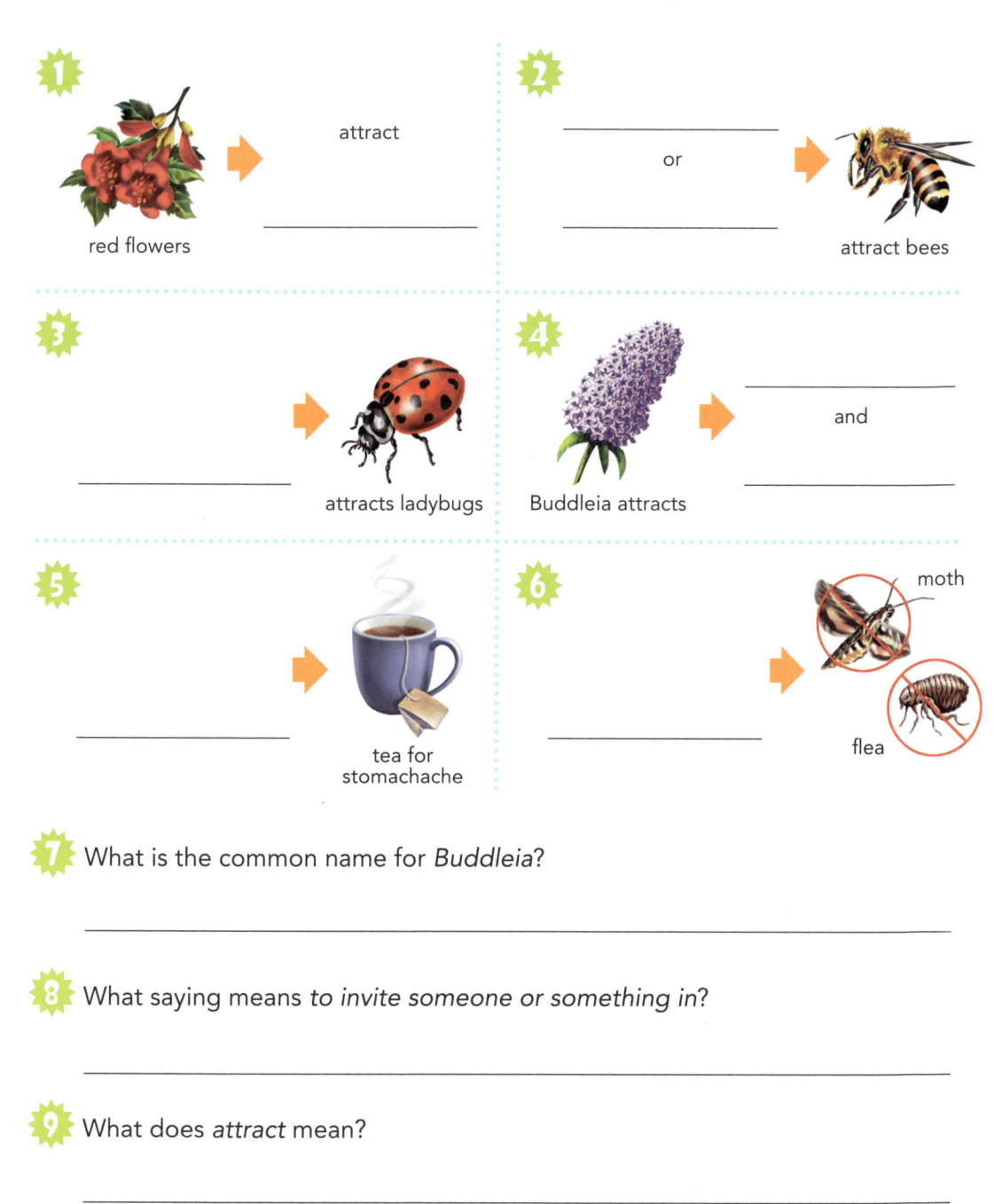

1 red flowers → attract _____

2 _____ or _____ → attract bees

3 _____ → attracts ladybugs

4 Buddleia attracts _____ and _____

5 _____ → tea for stomachache

6 _____ → moth / flea

7 What is the common name for *Buddleia*?

_____

8 What saying means *to invite someone or something in*?

_____

9 What does *attract* mean?

_____

© 2012 CTP - 7236

21

Stay Away!

Read the passage. Then answer the questions on page 23.

Just as some scents and plants will attract other living things, using certain perfumes or plants will also keep some creatures away. For years, farmers have used this knowledge to keep certain bugs and animals away from their crops. When creatures ruin crops, they are called pests. What can be planted to keep some of those pests away?

If rabbits or squirrels are a problem, then farmers will often sprinkle chili pepper. This has also inspired some people to sprinkle chili pepper, also called cayenne pepper, in their backyards to stop dogs from digging in the grass. The smell alone usually works in each situation.

If bugs are a problem, then farmers will often plant basil or rosemary bushes. In addition to being a natural repellant, rosemary will also smell wonderful and can be added to many recipes. Another tasty addition to recipes that comes from the garden is garlic. Adding garlic to a garden will also keep the moles, mice, and aphids away.

With the addition of certain plants, a garden or yard can be free of unwanted pests.

Stay Away!

Use the passage on page 22 to answer the questions.

1 **Problems:** _____ , _____ , or _____

   Solution: chili, or cayenne pepper

2 **Problem:** _____

   Solution: planting basil

3 **Problem:** _____

   Solution: planting rosemary

4 **Problem:** moles, mice, or aphids

   Solution: _____

5 What are pests?

   _____

6 Based on the passage on page 22 and what you know, what does the term *a natural repellant* mean?

   _____

   _____

7 How can someone keep pests out of a garden?

   _____

   _____

Penguins

Read the passage. Then answer the questions on page 25.

All penguins in the wild live in the southern hemisphere, but they don't all live in Antarctica. Contrary to what is shown in most popular books and movies, all penguins do not live in the snow. In fact, one type of penguin, the Galapagos penguin, lives off the west coast of South America on the equator!

All penguins do live near water, because they spend most of their time in the ocean. Because their legs are so far back on their bodies, it is hard for them to walk on land. Instead, they prefer to slide on their bellies across the ground or swim with their webbed feet. They may not be able to fly in the air, but their powerful flippers are used like boat oars to help them "fly" through the water. Their feet and tails help them steer. The body of a penguin is streamlined, meaning that it allows for smooth movement through water. Whether in the icy lands of Antarctica or the warm islands near the equator, penguins are unique birds that enjoy living in groups called colonies.

Penguins

Use the passage on page 24 to answer the questions.

1. Based on the context clues, what is the climate like near the equator?
   - a) icy
   - b) mild
   - c) warm

2. Based on the context clues, what would something that is *streamlined* do?
   - a) be as bumpy as a stream
   - b) create layers of water
   - c) make it harder to move through water
   - d) make it easier to move through water

3. What does it mean when it says they "fly" through the water?
   - a) They use their wings to fly through water.
   - b) They fly in and out of the water.
   - c) They move quickly.

4. Go back to the reading passage on page 24 and underline two words that would likely be in boldface print in a nonfiction book about penguins. Then use context clues to write the definition of each word on the lines below.

_____

_____

_____

_____

Pierre the Penguin

Read the passage. Then answer the questions on page 27.

Pierre, an African penguin, lived at the California Academy of Sciences with a group of other penguins and some scientists. He was their oldest penguin and a leader in the penguin colony. Pam Schaller, the aquatic biologist caring for Pierre, noticed that his feathers were slowly falling out, resulting in bald patches all over. She was so concerned for his health and well-being that she took him to the vet for many tests. None of the tests explained why he was going bald. Without his feathers to keep him warm, he was simply too cold to enter the water. The danger of hypothermia, life-threatening cold body temperature, was so large that Pierre had to watch his penguin friends and family enjoy the water without going in himself. Even worse, his penguin friends were picking on him because without his head feathers, they could not recognize him.

Pam needed to find a way for Pierre to swim again. His happiness, health, and safety depended on her ability to come up with a solution to this unusual problem. Since it had not occurred before, she had to invent some way for Pierre to stay warm. Thinking of her dog wearing a raincoat to stay warm, she wondered if Pierre could wear a wetsuit to stay warm in the water. After calling a wetsuit company and many design failures, they finally created a special wetsuit that worked. With his wetsuit, he was able to swim again! Even more amazing was the discovery that Pierre's feathers grew back six weeks later! Eventually, he was once again the leader of his penguin group.

Pierre the Penguin

Use the passage on page 26 to answer the questions.

1. What is the author's purpose?
- (a) entertain
- (b) persuade
- (c) inform

2. What is the theme of the story?
- (a) penguins can swim
- (b) penguins are special
- (c) penguins need feathers

3. What was the first problem that resulted from Pierre's feathers falling out?

_____

_____

4. What was the second problem that resulted from Pierre's feathers falling out?

_____

_____

5. What was the solution to Pierre's problem?

_____

_____

6. Based on information from the passage on page 26, did Pierre have to wear the wetsuit forever? Explain.

_____

_____

© 2012 CTP - 7236

How Chocolate Is Made

Read the passage. Then write the numbers 1–7 on the lines to put the steps in order.

Do you like the smell or taste of chocolate? Where does chocolate come from? It all begins when farmers plant cacao trees. Hard fruit, called pods, grow on the trees. Within each pod are seeds called cacao beans. After many months, farm workers cut the pods off the trees. The cacao beans are taken out of the pods, left out to dry in the sun for many days, and are then put into large sacks. The dried cacao beans are taken to a chocolate factory, where they are made into chocolate. First, the beans must be cleaned. Next, they are roasted, which means they are cooked. This helps the shells come off more easily. After the shells are removed, the beans are smashed into a soft paste called cocoa butter. To make the chocolate, milk and sugar are added to the cocoa butter and are mixed together for several days. By mixing it, the chocolate becomes smooth and creamy. Like putting water into ice trays, the chocolate is poured into trays to cool and harden. Next, the chocolate is removed from the trays and machines wrap the chocolate to be sold in stores. Now you know where chocolate comes from.

_____ cacao beans are cleaned and roasted

_____ shells are removed and beans are smashed

_____ cocoa beans dry in the sun

_____ farmers cut the pods off the trees and remove cocoa beans

_____ the milk, sugar, and cocoa butter are mixed and left to cool in trays

_____ farmers plant cocoa trees

_____ chocolate is removed from trays, wrapped, and sent to stores

A Happy Accident

Read the passage. Then answer the questions.

One day in 1930, Ruth Wakefield was baking her favorite butter drop cookies when she realized that she was out of chocolate. She had accidentally forgotten to get the baker's chocolate she needed for her recipe. As a substitute, she decided to chop up a chocolate bar. Although she had hoped the chopped up chocolate would melt into her dough, it actually made little chocolate chips in her cookies. That accident led to the creation of the famous chocolate chip cookie!

At the time, Ruth Wakefield owned an inn called the Toll House Inn. She passed out her accidental cookie "invention" to the people who stayed at her inn. They loved them! A cookie company heard of her creation and named their now famous chocolate chips after her inn. Her recipe is on the back of each bag of Toll House chocolate chips found at the store today. From an accident while baking cookies, many people are happily eating chocolate chip cookies today.

1. What was the author's purpose?
    a) entertain
    b) persuade
    c) inform

2. Chocolate chip cookies were accidentally "invented" by Ruth Wakefied.
    a) fact
    b) opinion

3. Everyone loves chocolate chip cookies.
    a) fact
    b) opinion

4. What was the effect of Ruth Wakefield not having the chocolate she needed to make her cookies?
   _____

5. Why do you think the recipe on the back of the chocolate chips is called the "Toll House Chocolate Chip Cookies"?
   _____
   _____

Jordan's Tundra Report

Read the passage. Then answer the questions.

The tundra is a biome in which there are very cold temperatures, strong winds, and snow that covers the ground most of the year. The harsh environment of the tundra explains why there are few things living there. The animals that do live in the tundra have adapted to the cold temperatures. Some mammals that live in the polar tundra include the polar bears, arctic foxes, and arctic hares. These polar tundra animals need to keep as much heat as possible in their bodies during the long winters, so they have thick fur coats. Their fur coats also help them blend in with their surroundings, which is called camouflage.

1. What makes the tundra a harsh environment?
   _____

2. What are three animals that live in the polar tundra?
   _____ _____ _____

3. What is camouflage?
   _____

Answer the following questions by making an inference based on the passage.

4. List one reason why an arctic hare needs camouflage.
   _____

5. Which season is long in the polar tundra?
   _____

6. Why do you think few people live in the tundra?
   _____

Siku the Polar Bear

Read the passage and the pages from Siku's Development Log. Then answer the questions.

Have you seen any of the videos of Siku on the Internet? Siku is a polar bear who was born on November 22, 2011, in Denmark. Since Siku is a mammal, he needed to drink milk to survive. His mother was unable to feed him, so he was cared for by the zookeepers at the Scandanavian Wildlife Park. The name Siku means "sea ice." Zookeepers gave him this name because they wanted to remind the world of the importance of taking care of the polar regions. Without sea ice, polar bears cannot survive. Siku was fed milk from a bottle, cared for 24 hours a day by a zookeeper, and taught how to act like a regular polar bear.

Siku's Development Log:

Day 1:   November 22, 2011 – Baby Siku is born! His eyes are closed.
Day 11: December 2, 2011 – Siku's eyes are still closed.
Day 16: December 7, 2011 – Siku tries to stand up. Eyes still closed.
Day 23: December 14, 2011 – Eyes open!
Day 32: December 23, 2011 – Siku enjoys massages from the zookeepers.
Day 37: December 28, 2011 – Siku gets weighed.
Day 44: January 4, 2012 – Siku's paws are measured after he finished a bottle of milk.

1 What caused Siku to be raised by the zookeepers?

2 What is the effect on polar bears of ice melting in the polar regions?

3 Why was Siku named after sea ice?

4 How long did it take Siku to open his eyes?

5 List two things that can be inferred as being important jobs of the zookeepers raising Siku?

Questioning Strategies

Read the information below. Then fill in the bubble beside the method that would most likely help you answer each question.

A good reader asks questions before, during, and after reading. The questions you ask yourself might include the following:

- *I wonder . . .*
- *Why wasn't . . .*
- *I thought . . .*
- *Where did it say that? Let me go back and find that.*

Questions you have while you read can be answered in one of four ways.
1. With background knowledge.
2. In the text itself. Look back, reread, or skim to find it.
3. Making inferences. Background knowledge + the clues in the book = the answer.
4. Conducting research. Search books or the Internet for the answer.

1. What was the first thing he did?
- ⓐ background knowledge
- ⓑ in the text
- ⓒ inference
- ⓓ research

2. Why did the grasshopper fly? I thought they only hopped.
- ⓐ background knowledge
- ⓑ in the text
- ⓒ inference
- ⓓ research

3. How did she get from the field to the door? The book only gives clues.
- ⓐ background knowledge
- ⓑ in the text
- ⓒ inference
- ⓓ research

4. When did that happen? It never said it in the book.
- ⓐ background knowledge
- ⓑ in the text
- ⓒ inference
- ⓓ research

5. Who took the cookie?
- ⓐ background knowledge
- ⓑ in the text
- ⓒ inference
- ⓓ research

The Missing Sandwich

Read the passage. Then go back and underline any clues in the text that help explain what happened to the sandwich. Then fill in the following graphic organizer to help you solve the mystery.

Ann was sure she had packed a sandwich in her lunch before leaving for her camping trip. When she and her friends arrived at the campground and set their table for lunch, she noticed a hole in her backpack. When she took her lunch out of her backpack, it came out in pieces. Her lunch bag was torn into pieces and only her thermos and apple sauce were still there. What could have happened to her lunch?

Ann tried to remember what she did between packing her lunch and leaving on her camping trip. She remembered making her peanut butter and jelly sandwich, putting it in a pouch, then placing it in her lunch bag after hugging her dog. Thinking back, she was sure she put the lunch in her backpack, gave her dog his favorite treat (peanut butter on her cutoff crust), then cleaned up her mess. The last thing she remembered doing was rushing to kiss everyone goodbye, hug her happy dog, and grab her backpack on her way to the car.

What was she missing or forgetting? Where was that sandwich?

Clues from text:	My background knowledge	My inference
	+	=

Amazing Amphibians

Read the passage. Then answer the questions.

Amphibians like wet places. Most amphibians live in or around water, which explains why their skin is smooth and wet. Most hatch and grow up in fresh water, such as ponds, streams, and rivers. When they are adults, they move onto dry land. What's amazing about amphibians is that most completely change their appearance as they grow. This change is called a metamorphosis. The frog is a good example. It changes from an egg to a tadpole, then a froglet, and finally a frog. The frog looks completely different from the egg and tadpole stages. Another amazing change involves how it breathes. As a tadpole, it breathes through gills. However, as a froglet, it develops lungs to breathe air. Isn't that amazing?

1 Where do amphibians live?
- (a) in water
- (b) on land
- (c) around water
- (d) a and c

2 What is a complete change in a life cycle called?
- (a) amphibian
- (b) transformation
- (c) metamorphosis
- (d) developing

3 What is the third stage of a frog's life cycle?
- (a) froglet
- (b) toad
- (c) frog
- (d) tadpole

4 What are two amazing facts about amphibians?

_____   _____

5 How would you find out the difference between frogs and toads?
- (a) background knowledge
- (b) inference
- (c) in the text
- (d) research

Marvelous Mammals

Read the passage. Then fill in the bubble beside the correct answer.

All mammals share the following characteristics: born alive, drink milk, breathe with lungs, and are covered with hair or fur. They are also all warm-blooded, meaning they can maintain their internal body temperature. The biggest mammal is the blue whale, while the smallest is the hog-nosed bat. Most swimming mammals have flippers and fins instead of legs. Bats are the only mammals that can fly. Mammals can be carnivores (meat eaters), herbivores (plant eaters), or omnivores (both meat and plant eaters). A few mammals eat only one or two kinds of foods. The giant panda eats mainly bamboo. The vampire bat eats only blood. You are a mammal. What do you eat?

1. Using context clues, what are carnivores?
   - (a) blood eaters
   - (b) plant eaters
   - (c) meat and plant eaters
   - (d) meat eaters

2. Using context clues, what are omnivores?
   - (a) blood eaters
   - (b) plant eaters
   - (c) meat and plant eaters
   - (d) meat eaters

3. What was the author's purpose?
   - (a) entertain
   - (b) inform
   - (c) persuade
   - (d) describe

4. Which of the following is an inference made after reading the passage?
   - (a) vampire bats eat only blood
   - (b) mammals breathe with lungs
   - (c) warm-blooded animals can maintain their internal body temperature
   - (d) giant pandas will be extinct when there is no bamboo left

5. As you were reading the passage, if you wondered what animals are herbivores, how would you find the answer?
   - (a) background knowledge
   - (b) inference
   - (c) in the text
   - (d) research

© 2012 CTP - 7236

Cause and Effect

Read the information in the box. Then draw a line to match each cause to its effect.

> A **cause** is something that makes something else happen.
> An **effect** is the result of something happening.
>
> The cause-effect relationship links events together. Many times, authors explain why something happened.

Causes

- falling asleep while laying on a beach chair at the beach on a sunny day
- not wearing safety equipment on a skateboard
- staying up 2 hours past bedtime
- forgetting to feed the dogs
- putting clothes in the dryer but forgetting to turn it on

Effects

- feeling very tired
- getting a bad sunburn
- knee was badly scraped after a fall
- having smelly, wet clothes
- having a shoe chewed

Important Inventions

Read the passage. Then answer the questions.

> Long before the Internet was invented, people were busy discovering ways to meet their needs. The ability to create fire came from a need to stay warm, have light, and cook food thousands of years ago. Now we have barbecues. The first wheels were invented out of a need to move things from one place to another more easily. Now we have cars. The first windmills were invented to grind grain. Today we have wind turbines to make electricity. The first writing involved pictures on clay tablets. Today we have e-mail, text messaging, and the Internet. The discoveries and inventions of the future will be based on the needs of today.

1. Which need led to the discovery of fire?
- (a) warmth
- (b) cook food
- (c) light
- (d) all of the above

2. Which need led to the invention of windmills?
- (a) movement
- (b) heat
- (c) grinding grain
- (d) electricity

3. Which need led to the invention of the wheel?
- (a) movement
- (b) heat
- (c) grinding grain
- (d) electricity

4. Had fire not been discovered, we would not have _____.

5. What three types of communication today began with writing on clay tablets many years ago?

_____   _____   _____

6. Why are things invented?

_____

Violent Volcanoes

Read the passage. Then answer the questions.

A volcano is a landform (usually a mountain) where hot, liquid rock bursts out of the earth. The liquid that is inside the volcano is called magma. The liquid that is seen flowing or shooting out during a volcanic eruption is called lava. The biggest eruptions are an effect of pressure building up underground. After the eruption, the lava cools into solid rock. The more lava that comes out of a volcano, the larger the volcano becomes as it cools. A volcano can even create a new island. In fact, the island of Surtsey was created in exactly that way. A volcano erupted at the bottom of the sea near Iceland in 1963. The lava and ash piled up so high that it went above sea level to create an island. Today, the island is covered by moss, grass, and trees, which provide homes for birds and insects.

1. What is the effect of built-up pressure underground?
    a) lava
    b) eruption
    c) magma
    d) landform

2. What is the effect of magma bursting out of the earth?
    a) lava flows or shoots up into the air
    b) lava cools into hard rock
    c) an island is formed
    d) an earthquake

3. What do you think happens to grass and trees in the path of the lava?

_____

4. Why do you think there are no people living on the island of Surtsey even though it has been there for over 60 years?

_____

Omnilife Stadium

Read the passage. Then answer the questions.

On July 29, 2010, a new and unique soccer stadium opened in Guadalajara, Mexico. The design was inspired by volcanoes. It even has a white roof cover designed to look like a large cloud over the seats. The sides of the stadium look like a mountain and are covered with grass. It was built by many different companies to be "green," meaning it uses technology that does not harm the earth. For example, the roof collects rainfall to be cleaned and used for watering and cleaning. The grass is not real. Instead, it is made out of sand and recycled sports shoes. From far away, the Omnilife Stadium really does look like a volcano.

1. What does it mean for a building to be "green"?
   _____

2. How is the Omnilife Stadium "green"?
   _____

3. Why do you think they built it in the shape of a volcano?
   _____

4. Why do you think the designers wanted the stadium to be "green"?
   _____

5. Why is it good that the stadium's roof collects rainwater?
   _____

6. How is the stadium's grass "green"?
   _____

Super Soccer Facts

Read the facts. Then answer the questions.

1. Soccer is the most popular team sport.
2. Penalties against an opposing team include pushing, tripping, holding, and charging from behind.
3. A single soccer player runs about 7 miles during an entire game.
4. Soccer is called "football" in nearly every country, except in the United States and Canada.
5. The World Cup, held every four years, is the biggest soccer tournament in the world.
6. Soccer is the fastest growing college and high school sport in the United States.
7. The standard soccer ball is made out of leather.

1 What is the World Cup? _____

How often is it held? _____

2 What does fact number three tell you about the fitness of soccer players?

_____

3 What would happen if someone pushed another player during a soccer game?

_____

4 Which fact from the list above is the only fact a person would need to know while playing a game of soccer?

_____

_____

Making Connections

Read the passage. Then fill in the bubble beside the correct answer.

There are many different reasons for reading. Perhaps you are trying to gather information, learn something new, or simply laugh. The goal of reading is to understand what is read. To help your brain remember what you read, it tries to make connections between what you are reading and something you already know.

There are three main types of connections your brain makes while reading. A **text-to-text** connection happens when your brain compares what you are reading to something you have already read. It might sound like this, "That reminds me of the story I read last week." A **text-to-self** connection involves thinking about how the story or book relates to you. It might sound like this, "I went skiing in the mountains just like the main character." A **text-to-world** connection involves thinking about something you have heard or seen in the world and how it relates to what you are reading. An example of this might be reading a book about volcanoes and thinking, "I just saw that there was a volcanic eruption in Hawaii on the news yesterday."

Smart readers make connections to other reading materials, the world, and their experiences.

1. While reading a story about a magician, you are reminded of the magic show you saw last week. What type of connection did you make?
   - a) text-to-text
   - b) text-to-self
   - c) text-to-world

2. While reading a scientific article about the planet Mars, you wonder what it might be like to travel to the red planet. What type of connection did you make?
   - a) text-to-text
   - b) text-to-self
   - c) text-to-world

3. While reading a book about the president, you are reminded of the notes you took while reading your social studies textbook. What type of connection did you make?
   - a) text-to-text
   - b) text-to-self
   - c) text-to-world

Hopping Along

Read the passage to help you answer the questions below. Then complete the Venn diagram on page 43.

What animal pops into your head when you think of an animal that hops? Is it a rabbit or a kangaroo? The physical features of rabbits and kangaroos are similar in many ways. They both have tall ears that usually point straight up; large hind legs to help them hop; and fur covering their skin. Those same three features also have differences. While a kangaroo's ears go up, a rabbit's ears can be up or down depending on the species. Although they both have larger hind legs than front legs, the front legs of the kangaroo are too short to touch the ground as it hops. Finally, kangaroos have a special skin-lined pouch in which a joey, a baby kangaroo, will grow and be protected. Rabbits do not have a pouch. They may look similar as they hop along, but a closer look shows you the many differences between rabbits and kangaroos.

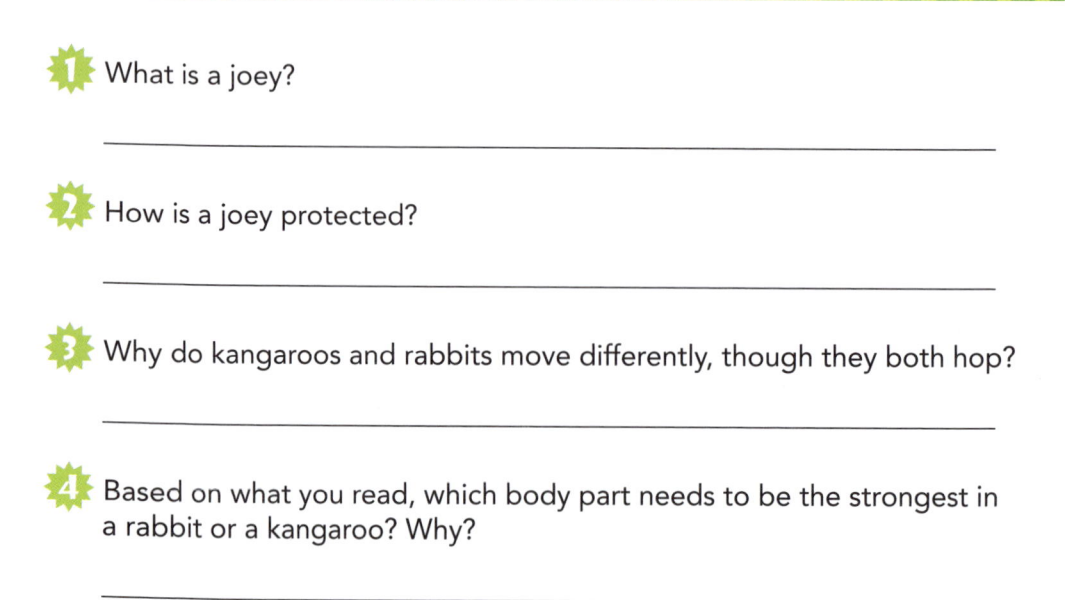

1 What is a joey?

_____

2 How is a joey protected?

_____

3 Why do kangaroos and rabbits move differently, though they both hop?

_____

4 Based on what you read, which body part needs to be the strongest in a rabbit or a kangaroo? Why?

_____

Hopping Along

Use the passage on page 42 to write at least three items in each section of the Venn diagram.

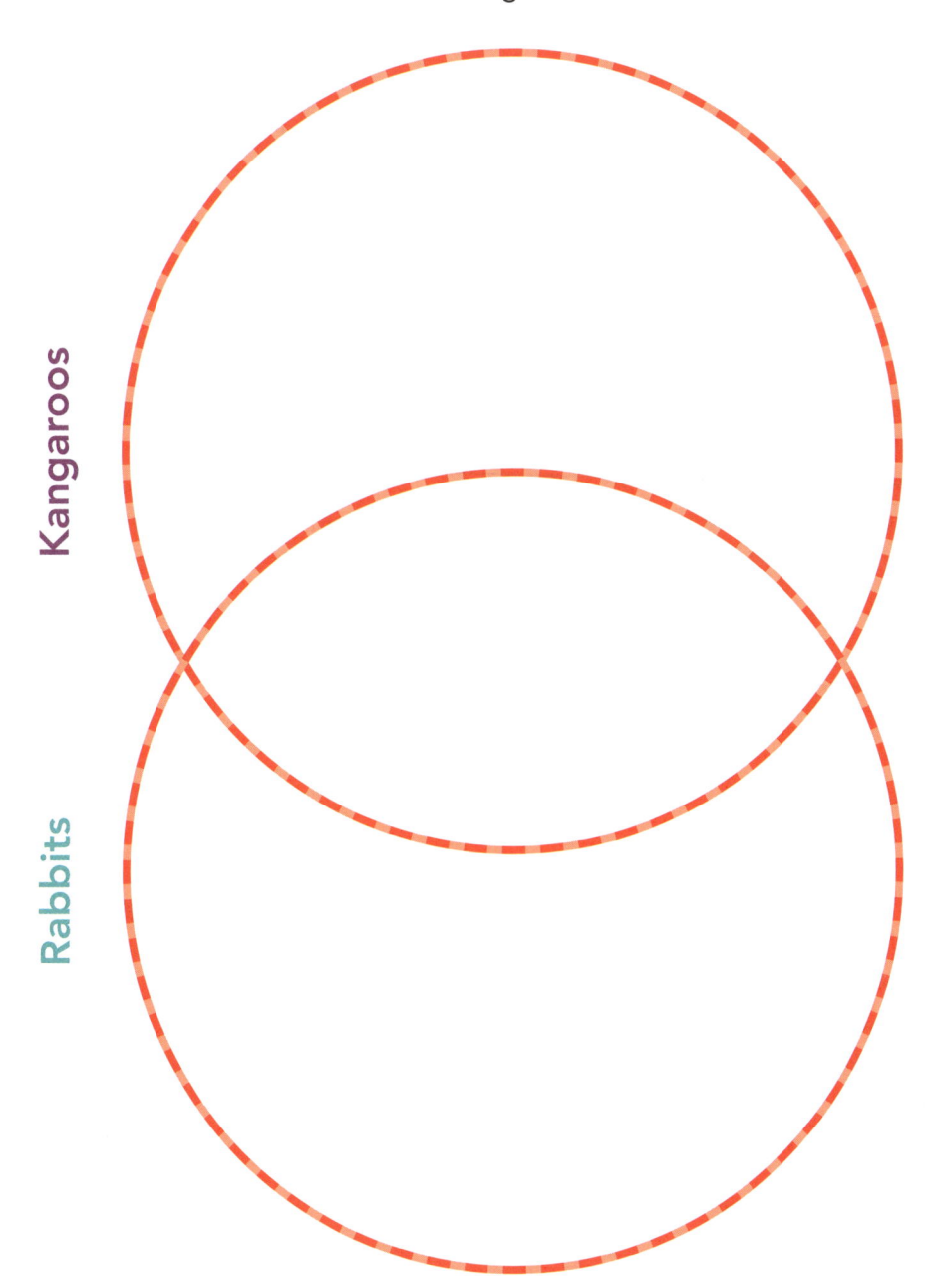

Kangaroos

Rabbits

Hamburger or Pizza?

Read the passage. Then answer the questions.

Two of the most popular foods are hamburgers and pizzas. At first glance, they look completely different. However, there are three ways in which hamburgers and pizzas are surprisingly similar. First, they both require something to hold the ingredients. A pizza needs some type of crust for the toppings to be layered upon. A hamburger needs some type of bun or wrap to hold the ingredients. The second way they are similar is the most commonly added topping: cheese. Speaking of toppings, that is the third way they are similar. Both hamburgers and pizzas can be customized in hundreds of different ways. Some popular variations of hamburgers include the double cheeseburger, Cajun burger, and the Aloha burger. Popular pizzas include the barbecue chicken pizza, the meat lovers pizza, and the Hawaiian pizza. Now you know that, while they may look different, hamburgers and pizzas are similar foods.

1 List three ways that hamburgers and pizzas are similar.

_____

_____

_____

2 What is the most common ingredient in both hamburgers and pizzas?
- (a) meat
- (b) lettuce or vegetables
- (c) cheese
- (d) tomatoes

3 Which ingredients would an Aloha burger and a Hawaiian pizza most likely have in common?
- (a) pineapple
- (b) seaweed
- (c) hamburger meat
- (d) spinach

4 What does the word *customized* most likely mean in the third example?
- (a) eaten
- (b) sold
- (c) cooked
- (d) designed

How to Make a Pizza Burger

Read the recipe. Then fill in the bubble beside the correct answer.

Prep time: 15 minutes   **Cook time:** 10 minutes
Yield: a dozen ¼ pound burgers   **Difficulty level:** Easy

Ingredients:
- 3 pounds hamburger meat
- ½ teaspoon of each: oregano, basil, garlic powder
- 1 small onion
- 1 small green or red pepper chopped into small pieces
- ½ cup pizza sauce
- 12 slices mozzarella cheese
- 12 slices provolone cheese
- 12 slices pepperoni
- 12 buns

Directions:
1. Mix the meat, spices, onion, and pepper pieces together.
2. Shape them into hamburger patties.
3. Grill for 10 minutes or until completely cooked.
4. Spread pizza sauce on buns.
5. Put a hamburger, a slice of each cheese, and pepperoni in each bun.

1 What do you need to do first?
 a. add pizza sauce to the meat
 b. grill the buns
 c. shape the burgers

2 What does the word "yield" most likely mean?
 a. cook
 b. make room on the barbecue
 c. the amount made

3 What does "prep time" most likely mean?
 a. how long it takes to grill
 b. how long it takes to prepare the ingredients
 c. how long it has to cool

© 2012 CTP - 7236

Essay Contest Winner: Proud to Be a Junior Lifeguard!

Read the passage. Then answer the questions.

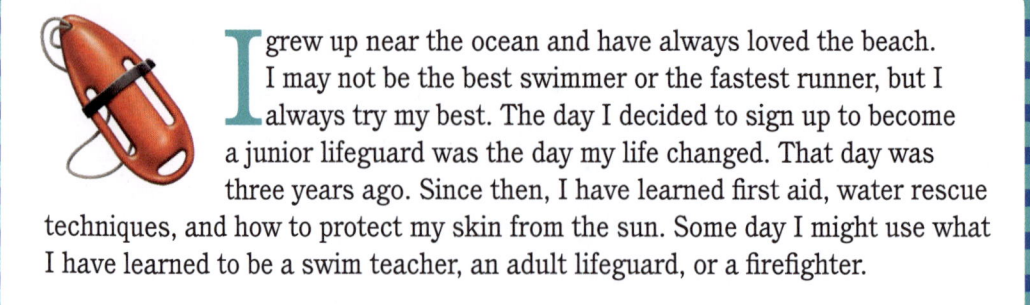

I grew up near the ocean and have always loved the beach. I may not be the best swimmer or the fastest runner, but I always try my best. The day I decided to sign up to become a junior lifeguard was the day my life changed. That day was three years ago. Since then, I have learned first aid, water rescue techniques, and how to protect my skin from the sun. Some day I might use what I have learned to be a swim teacher, an adult lifeguard, or a firefighter.

1. What are three things that a junior lifeguard learns?

_____

_____

_____

2. What is true?
- (a) You must be the best swimmer.
- (b) You must be willing to try your best.
- (c) You must be the fastest runner.
- (d) You must be able to hold your breath for 30 seconds.

3. Look at question 2 above. Which answer choice was not even mentioned in the winning essay?

_____

4. What was the author's purpose?
- (a) inform
- (b) entertain
- (c) persuade
- (d) describe

5. What can you infer about becoming a junior lifeguard based on the essay?
- (a) You must be able to swim.
- (b) You must be able to hold your breath underwater at least 30 seconds.
- (c) You must be at least 12 years old.
- (d) You must first pass a first aid test.

First Aid Kits

Read the lists. Then fill in the bubble beside the correct answer.

Kit 1 Supplies:
- tweezers
- burn gel
- bandages
- antiseptic wipes
- cotton balls

Kit 2 Supplies:
- emergency blanket
- flashlight
- waterproof matches
- scissors
- battery-powered radio

1. What is most likely the purpose of Kit 1?
   - ⓐ earthquake/tornado emergency kit
   - ⓑ eye injury kit
   - ⓒ simple accident kit
   - ⓓ bee sting kit

2. What is most likely the purpose of Kit 2?
   - ⓐ earthquake/tornado emergency kit
   - ⓑ eye injury kit
   - ⓒ simple accident kit
   - ⓓ bee sting kit

3. In a house, where should Kit 1 be stored?
   - ⓐ kitchen
   - ⓑ garage
   - ⓒ bathroom
   - ⓓ all of the above

4. Other than in a house, where could a family store Kit 2?
   - ⓐ mailbox
   - ⓑ purse
   - ⓒ car trunk
   - ⓓ all of the above

5. If a family wanted to be prepared for different types of emergencies, which Kit should they buy?
   - ⓐ Kit 1
   - ⓑ Kits 1 and 2
   - ⓒ Kit 2
   - ⓓ neither kit

Tricky Expressions

Read the passage. Then read the information in the chart below that explains some common idioms. Then complete page 49.

> Are you as smart as a whip? Is this a piece of cake? Do you get a kick out of all of this? Maybe you know every trick in the book to convince someone to listen to you, but perhaps sometimes you feel like your hands are tied.
>
> If the paragraph above was tricky to understand, then you know how expressions called *idioms* can affect reading. Idioms are phrases that mean something totally different from the words themselves. Many authors use idioms as if everyone understands them, but idioms are often quite tricky.

Types of Idioms	Examples
colors	green with envy; out of the blue; silver lining
animals	clam up; in the doghouse; hold your horses
foods	piece of cake; in a nutshell; sweet tooth
actions	blow the whistle; draw the line; bite your tongue
get or keep	get off the hook; get a kick out of it; get cold feet
similes	as smart as a whip; like a fish out of water; as cold as ice
metaphors	hands are tied; spill the beans; hard to swallow
hyperbole	made my head spin; every trick in the book; talking his head off

Not So Tricky Anymore!

Use the context clues and the chart on page 48 to fill in the bubble beside the meaning of each idiom underlined below.

1. When Pat's sister got a new bike, but Pat got her sister's old bike, Pat was feeling <u>green with envy</u>.
   - ⓐ happy
   - ⓑ helpful
   - ⓒ jealous
   - ⓓ important

2. When Kari was running down the hall ahead of the class, her teacher said, "<u>Hold your horses!</u>"
   - ⓐ you're first
   - ⓑ hold on tight
   - ⓒ run faster
   - ⓓ slow down

3. Mario said, "I can ride a scooter. It's a <u>piece of cake</u>!"
   - ⓐ sweet
   - ⓑ easy
   - ⓒ small
   - ⓓ colorful

4. Jack had to <u>bite his tongue</u> in the meeting so he would not say something he might regret later.
   - ⓐ be quiet
   - ⓑ open his mouth
   - ⓒ bite harder
   - ⓓ eat quickly

5. Anna got <u>cold feet</u> when it came time to perform in front of the crowd.
   - ⓐ forgot her shoes
   - ⓑ got nervous
   - ⓒ got excited
   - ⓓ fell in the water

6. Art felt like a <u>fish out of water</u> in his new school.
   - ⓐ out of place
   - ⓑ excited
   - ⓒ wet
   - ⓓ smart

7. Erin did not <u>spill the beans</u>, so Fred was really surprised!
   - ⓐ tell a secret
   - ⓑ pay the bill
   - ⓒ answer
   - ⓓ show up late

8. Silvia knew <u>every trick in the book</u> when it came to helping kids feel better.
   - ⓐ magic tricks
   - ⓑ each book
   - ⓒ every way
   - ⓓ the words

© 2012 CTP - 7236

I'm Getting Braces

Read the passage, including the words under the lines. Then complete the activity on page 51.

Mom said, "Come on, it's time to go!" Of course, I was _____(1)_____.
                                                          delaying
I really didn't want to get braces on my teeth. In fact, I was really _____(2)_____ about the whole thing. I had _____(3)_____ about
              sad   a nervous feeling in my stomach
having wires put on my teeth. My mom came over to give me a hug. She said, "Don't worry! It's _____(4)_____. It'll be over _____(5)_____.
                                                  easy   soon
You'll only be wearing these braces until next year." I didn't want to get _____(6)_____ for not brushing my teeth as well as I should, but it was time
         in trouble
_____(7)_____.
     to go

When we got to the office, Dr. Shen started talking about what he would be doing. It was all going _____(8)_____ as I was busy thinking about
                                          by me without me hearing it
how much it might hurt. Then he said, "Let's _____(9)_____." That got my
                                                      start
attention. I knew I would have to _____(10)_____ and give in. I was getting
                                         be strong
braces whether I liked it or not.

I _____(11)_____ that it wouldn't hurt and closed my eyes. For a
       hoped
minute I thought, "I could _____(12)_____ by asking questions." Instead, I
                                  stall
was _____(13)_____ as he went to work. In no time, the braces were on my
        silent
teeth. Dr. Shen said, "Look! We're already done."_____(14)_____," I thought.
                                                        That was fast

My mom handed me a mirror from her purse and said, "You look great! I bet it didn't hurt a bit!" Actually it did, but I _____(15)_____. After all, it was
                                                              stayed quiet
over and the braces were on. I did look pretty good, and I knew my teeth would be much straighter very soon.

50 © 2012 CTP - 7236

I'm Getting Braces

Write the correct letters on the lines to match the numbered words from the passage on page 50 to the correct idiom. Then reread the passage on page 50 with the idioms included.

1. delaying _____
2. sad _____
3. a nervous feeling in my stomach _____
4. easy _____
5. soon _____
6. in trouble _____
7. to go _____
8. by me without me hearing it _____
9. start _____
10. be strong _____
11. hoped _____
12. stall _____
13. silent _____
14. That was fast _____
15. stayed quiet _____

a. in no time
b. feeling blue
c. get this show on the road
d. putting it off
e. as quiet as a mouse
f. drag my feet
g. held my tongue
h. Time flies when we're having fun
i. kept my fingers crossed
j. in one ear and out the other
k. to get going
l. chewed out
m. a piece of cake
n. pull myself together
o. butterflies in my stomach

© 2012 CTP - 7236

51

Cumulative Quiz

Congratulations! You know the strategies and skills that hold the keys to great reading comprehension! Fill in the bubble beside the correct answer.

1. Which genre is *least* likely to relate to events that took place in real life?
- a) biography
- b) informational
- c) fantasy
- d) autobiography

2. What is the main purpose of most nonfiction books?
- a) entertain
- b) inform
- c) describe
- d) persuade

3. When do good readers make inferences?
- a) before reading
- b) after reading
- c) while they read
- d) all of the above

4. The result of an event is called the _____.
- a) cause
- b) effect
- c) problem
- d) inference

5. When you try to tell someone what a story was all about in only a few sentences, then you are trying to tell the _____.
- a) sequence
- b) author's purpose
- c) details
- d) main idea

6. When you figure out the meaning of an unknown word by reading around the word to find a synonym, antonym, definition, description, or summary, what strategy are you using?
- a) making connections
- b) context clues
- c) using background knowledge
- d) visualizing

7. The most important goal of reading anything is _____.
- a) comprehending
- b) writing a response
- c) answering questions
- d) passing a test

Answer Key

PAGE 3

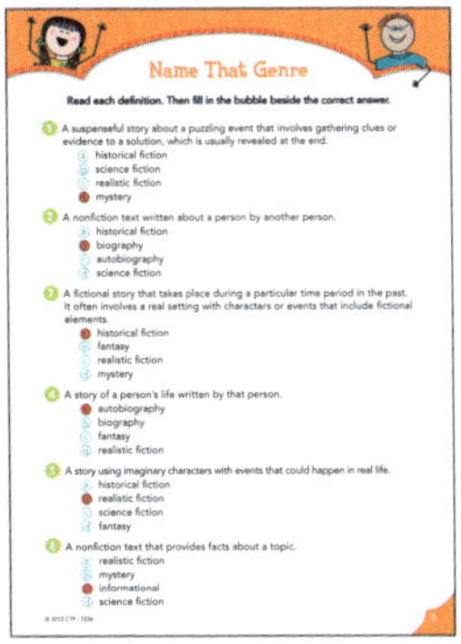

Name That Genre

Read each definition. Then fill in the bubble beside the correct answer.

1. A suspenseful story about a puzzling event that involves gathering clues or evidence to a solution, which is usually revealed at the end.
   - a. historical fiction
   - b. science fiction
   - c. realistic fiction
   - ● mystery
2. A nonfiction text written about a person by another person.
   - a. historical fiction
   - ● biography
   - c. autobiography
   - d. science fiction
3. A fictional story that takes place during a particular time period in the past. It often involves a real setting with characters or events that include fictional elements.
   - ● historical fiction
   - b. fantasy
   - c. realistic fiction
   - d. mystery
4. A story of a person's life written by that person.
   - ● autobiography
   - b. biography
   - c. fantasy
   - d. realistic fiction
5. A story using imaginary characters with events that could happen in real life.
   - a. historical fiction
   - ● realistic fiction
   - c. science fiction
   - d. fantasy
6. A nonfiction text that provides facts about a topic.
   - a. realistic fiction
   - b. mystery
   - ● informational
   - d. science fiction

PAGE 4

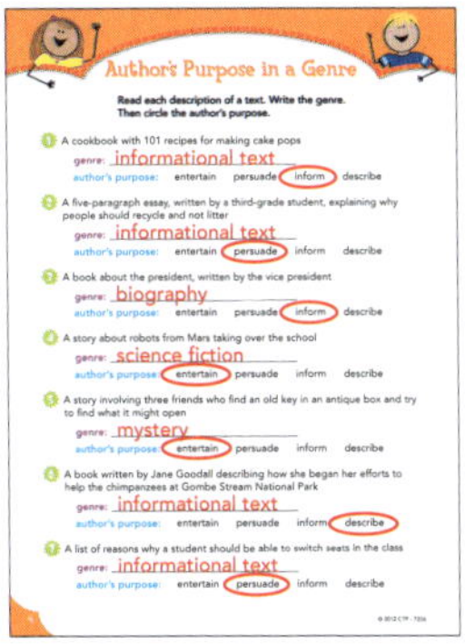

Author's Purpose in a Genre

Read each description of a text. Write the genre. Then circle the author's purpose.

1. A cookbook with 101 recipes for making cake pops
   genre: informational text
   author's purpose: entertain persuade **(inform)** describe
2. A five-paragraph essay, written by a third-grade student, explaining why people should recycle and not litter
   genre: informational text
   author's purpose: entertain **(persuade)** inform describe
3. A book about the president, written by the vice president
   genre: biography
   author's purpose: entertain persuade **(inform)** describe
4. A story about robots from Mars taking over the school
   genre: science fiction
   author's purpose: **(entertain)** persuade inform describe
5. A story involving three friends who find an old key in an antique box and try to find what it might open
   genre: mystery
   author's purpose: **(entertain)** persuade inform describe
6. A book written by Jane Goodall describing how she began her efforts to help the chimpanzees at Gombe Stream National Park
   genre: informational text
   author's purpose: entertain persuade inform **(describe)**
7. A list of reasons why a student should be able to switch seats in the class
   genre: informational text
   author's purpose: entertain **(persuade)** inform describe

PAGE 5

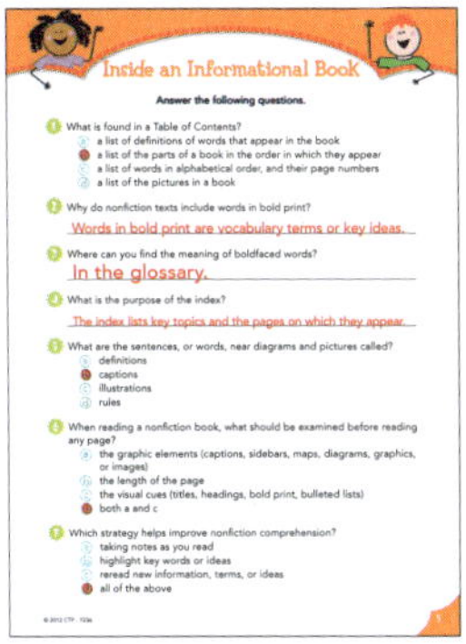

Inside an Informational Book

Answer the following questions.

1. What is found in a Table of Contents?
   - a. a list of definitions of words that appear in the book
   - ● a list of the parts of a book in the order in which they appear
   - c. a list of words in alphabetical order, and their page numbers
   - d. a list of the pictures in a book
2. Why do nonfiction texts include words in bold print?
   Words in bold print are vocabulary terms or key ideas.
3. Where can you find the meaning of boldfaced words?
   In the glossary.
4. What is the purpose of the index?
   The index lists key topics and the pages on which they appear.
5. What are the sentences, or words, near diagrams and pictures called?
   - a. definitions
   - ● captions
   - c. illustrations
   - d. rules
6. When reading a nonfiction book, what should be examined before reading any page?
   - a. the graphic elements (captions, sidebars, maps, diagrams, graphics, or images)
   - b. the length of the page
   - c. the visual cues (titles, headings, bold print, bulleted lists)
   - ● both a and c
7. Which strategy helps improve nonfiction comprehension?
   - a. taking notes as you read
   - b. highlight key words or ideas
   - c. reread new information, terms, or ideas
   - ● all of the above

PAGE 6

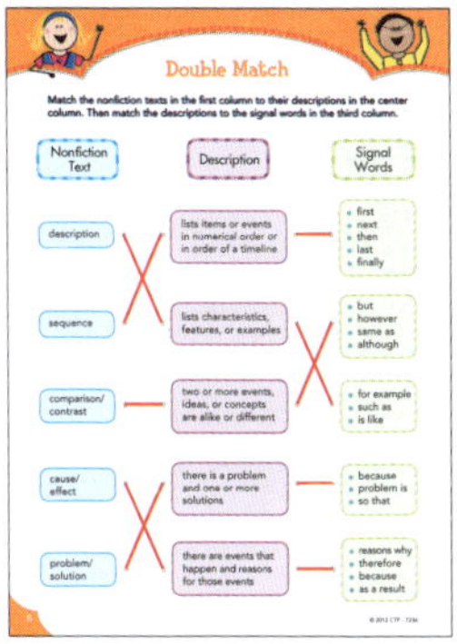

Double Match

Match the nonfiction texts in the first column to their descriptions in the center column. Then match the descriptions to the signal words in the third column.

Nonfiction Text	Description	Signal Words
description	lists items or events in numerical order or in order of a timeline	first, next, then, last, finally
sequence	lists characteristics, features, or examples	but, however, same as, although
comparison/contrast	two or more events, ideas, or concepts are alike or different	for example, such as, is like
cause/effect	there is a problem and one or more solutions	because, problem is, so that
problem/solution	there are events that happen and reasons for those events	reasons why, therefore, because, as a result

PAGE 7

Fact or Opinion?

Read the sentences below. Write F for fact and O for opinion.

1. O Making an ice cave is hard work.
2. F A bicycle has two wheels.
3. O Elephants are the most interesting animals to study.
4. O Zookeepers have the best jobs.
5. F Wearing a helmet keeps a person safer on a motorcycle.
6. O Everyone should wear kneepads when learning to ride a bike.
7. O Earning an allowance is an important way for children to learn about money.
8. O Hurricanes are scary.
9. O Swimming is the best Olympic event.
10. F Fog is a thick cloud close to the surface of the earth.

PAGE 8

More Fact and Opinion

Fill in the bubble beside the correct answer.

1. Which form of writing would most likely have more opinions than facts?
   - a. how-to article
   - ● letter to a friend
   - c. report
   - d. news story
2. Which form of writing would have only facts?
   - a. persuasive essay
   - b. letter to a friend
   - ● report
   - d. mystery
3. Which form of writing could have both facts and opinions?
   - ● persuasive essay
   - b. mystery
   - c. report
   - d. how-to article
4. Select the title of the magazine article that would likely have more facts than opinions.
   - a. "Reasons Why I Think Carrots are the Best Vegetable"
   - b. "Dancing Is Fun!"
   - ● "The Destruction of the Rain Forest"
   - d. "My Worst Vacation Ever"

PAGE 9

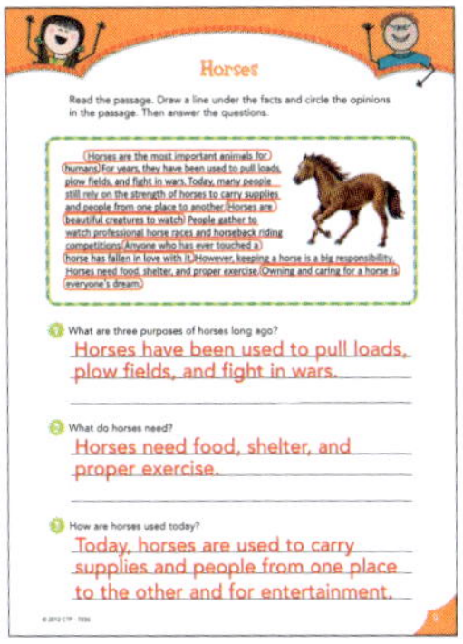

Horses

Read the passage. Draw a line under the facts and circle the opinions in the passage. Then answer the questions.

Horses are the most important animals for humans. For years, they have been used to pull loads, plow fields, and fight in wars. Today, many people still rely on the strength of horses to carry supplies and people from one place to another. Horses are beautiful creatures to watch. People gather to watch professional horse races and horseback riding competitions. Anyone who has ever touched a horse has fallen in love with it. However, keeping a horse is a big responsibility. Horses need food, shelter, and proper exercise. Owning and caring for a horse is everyone's dream.

1. What are three purposes of horses long ago?
   Horses have been used to pull loads, plow fields, and fight in wars.
2. What do horses need?
   Horses need food, shelter, and proper exercise.
3. How are horses used today?
   Today, horses are used to carry supplies and people from one place to the other and for entertainment.

PAGE 10

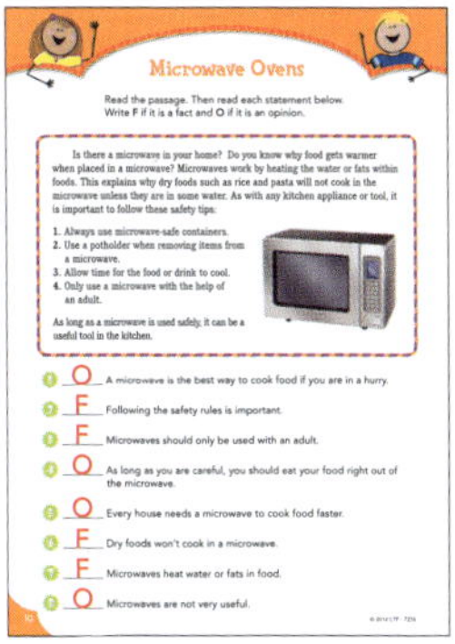

Microwave Ovens

Read the passage. Then read each statement below. Write F if it is a fact and O if it is an opinion.

Is there a microwave in your home? Do you know why food gets warmer when placed in a microwave? Microwaves work by heating the water or fats within foods. This explains why dry foods such as rice and pasta will not cook in the microwave unless they are in some water. As with any kitchen appliance or tool, it is important to follow these safety tips:

1. Always use microwave-safe containers.
2. Use a potholder when removing items from a microwave.
3. Allow time for the food or drink to cool.
4. Only use a microwave with the help of an adult.

As long as a microwave is used safely, it can be a useful tool in the kitchen.

1. O A microwave is the best way to cook food if you are in a hurry.
2. F Following the safety rules is important.
3. F Microwaves should only be used with an adult.
4. O As long as you are careful, you should eat your food right out of the microwave.
5. O Every house needs a microwave to cook food faster.
6. F Dry foods won't cook in a microwave.
7. F Microwaves heat water or fats in food.
8. O Microwaves are not very useful.

PAGE 11

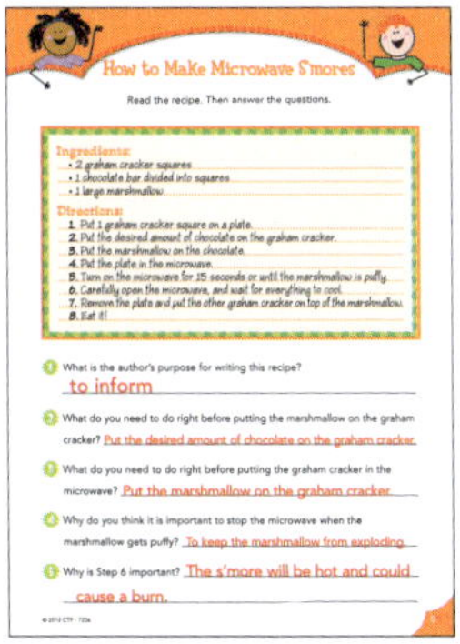

How to Make Microwave S'mores

Read the recipe. Then answer the questions.

Ingredients:
- 2 graham cracker squares
- 1 chocolate bar divided into squares
- 1 large marshmallow

Directions:
1. Put 1 graham cracker square on a plate.
2. Put the desired amount of chocolate on the graham cracker.
3. Put the marshmallow on the chocolate.
4. Put the plate in the microwave.
5. Turn on the microwave for 15 seconds or until the marshmallow is puffy.
6. Carefully open the microwave, and wait for everything to cool.
7. Remove the plate and put the other graham cracker on top of the marshmallow.
8. Eat it!

1. What is the author's purpose for writing this recipe?
   to inform
2. What do you need to do right before putting the marshmallow on the graham cracker? Put the desired amount of chocolate on the graham cracker.
3. What do you need to do right before putting the graham cracker in the microwave? Put the marshmallow on the graham cracker.
4. Why do you think it is important to stop the microwave when the marshmallow gets puffy? To keep the marshmallow from exploding.
5. Why is Step 6 important? The s'more will be hot and could cause a burn.

PAGE 12

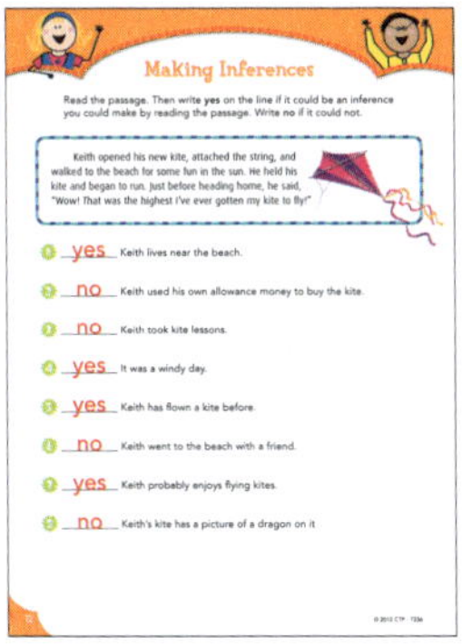

Making Inferences

Read the passage. Then write **yes** on the line if it could be an inference you could make by reading the passage. Write **no** if it could not.

Keith opened his new kite, attached the string, and walked to the beach for some fun in the sun. He held his kite and began to run. Just before heading home, he said, "Wow! That was the highest I've ever gotten my kite to fly!"

1. yes Keith lives near the beach.
2. no Keith used his own allowance money to buy the kite.
3. no Keith took kite lessons.
4. yes It was a windy day.
5. yes Keith has flown a kite before.
6. no Keith went to the beach with a friend.
7. yes Keith probably enjoys flying kites.
8. no Keith's kite has a picture of a dragon on it.

PAGE 13

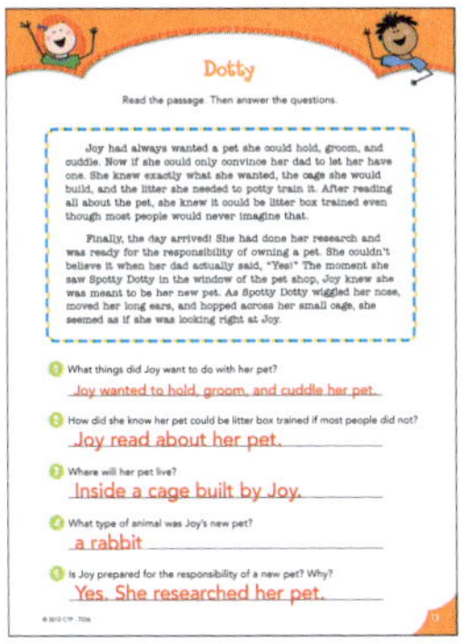

Dotty

Read the passage. Then answer the questions.

Joy had always wanted a pet she could hold, groom, and cuddle. Now if she could only convince her dad to let her have one. She knew exactly what she wanted, the cage she would build, and the litter she needed to potty train it. After reading all about the pet, she knew it could be litter box trained even though most people would never imagine that.

Finally, the day arrived! She had done her research and was ready for the responsibility of owning a pet. She couldn't believe it when her dad actually said, "Yes!" The moment she saw Spotty Dotty in the window of the pet shop, Joy knew she was meant to be her new pet. As Spotty Dotty wiggled her nose, moved her long ears, and hopped across her small cage, she seemed as if she was looking right at Joy.

1. What things did Joy want to do with her pet?
   Joy wanted to hold, groom, and cuddle her pet.
2. How did she know her pet could be litter box trained if most people did not?
   Joy read about her pet.
3. Where will her pet live?
   Inside a cage built by Joy.
4. What type of animal was Joy's new pet?
   a rabbit
5. Is Joy prepared for the responsibility of a new pet? Why?
   Yes. She researched her pet.

PAGE 14

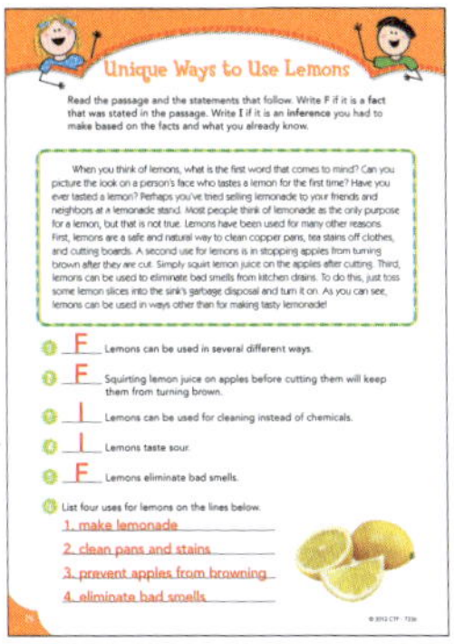

Unique Ways to Use Lemons

Read the passage and the statements that follow. Write F if it is a **fact** that was stated in the passage. Write I if it is an **inference** you had to make based on the facts and what you already know.

When you think of lemons, what is the first word that comes to mind? Can you picture the look on a person's face who tastes a lemon for the first time? Have you ever tasted a lemon? Perhaps you've tried selling lemonade to your friends and neighbors at a lemonade stand. Most people think of lemonade as the only purpose for a lemon, but that is not true. Lemons have been used for many other reasons. First, lemons are a safe and natural way to clean copper pans, tea stains off clothes, and cutting boards. A second use for lemons is in stopping apples from turning brown after they are cut. Simply squirt lemon juice on the apples after cutting. Third, lemons can be used to eliminate bad smells from kitchen drains. To do this, just toss some lemon slices into the sink's garbage disposal and turn it on. As you can see, lemons can be used in ways other than for making tasty lemonade!

1. F Lemons can be used in several different ways.
2. F Squirting lemon juice on apples before cutting them will keep them from turning brown.
3. I Lemons can be used for cleaning instead of chemicals.
4. I Lemons taste sour.
5. F Lemons eliminate bad smells.
6. List four uses for lemons on the lines below.
   1. make lemonade
   2. clean pans and stains
   3. prevent apples from browning
   4. eliminate bad smells

PAGE 15

How to Make Lemonade

Read the recipe. Then answer the following questions.

Prep time: 10 minutes **Yield:** 6 cups **Difficulty level:** Easy

Ingredients:
- 1 cup sugar
- 1 cup water
- juice from 6 lemons
- 4 cups of cold water

Directions:
1. Heat the sugar and water in a pot until the sugar dissolves to make sugar water.
2. Squeeze the juice from 6 lemons into a pitcher.
3. Add the sugar water to the pitcher.
4. Add the cold water.
5. Cool for 30 to 40 minutes in the refrigerator.
6. Serve with ice.

1. What do you need to do first to make lemonade?
   - (a) squeeze the lemons
   - (b) take out the ice
   - **(c) make sugar water**
2. What do you do before adding the cold water?
   - (a) cool in the refrigerator
   - **(b) add sugar water**
   - (c) add ice
3. What do you do after squeezing the juice from the lemons?
   - **(a) mix with sugar water**
   - (b) cool for 30 to 40 minutes
   - (c) squeeze 6 lemons
4. What do you think would happen to the lemonade if you squeezed 12 lemons instead of 6?
   The lemonade would be more sour.
5. How do you think the lemonade would be different if you used 3 cups of sugar instead of 1?
   The lemonade would be sweeter.

PAGE 16

Police Officers

Read the passage. Then read each statement below and fill in the bubble beside the answer that shows how the statement relates to the passage.

Have you ever thought about being a police officer some day? Perhaps you have seen one on the road or in a store. What exactly does a police officer do in a community? A police officer has many important roles related to enforcing the laws and keeping people safe. To be a police officer, a person needs to be healthy, honest, and have other good character traits.

1. A police officer needs to drive a car or motorcycle.
   - (a) in the text
   - (b) can be inferred from the text as true
   - (c) can be inferred from the text as false
   - **(d) cannot be inferred from the text and needs further research**
2. Being responsible and trustworthy are characteristics of police officers.
   - (a) in the text
   - **(b) can be inferred from the text as true**
   - (c) can be inferred from the text as false
   - (d) cannot be inferred from the text and needs further research
3. Police officers are community helpers who keep people safe.
   - **(a) in the text**
   - (b) can be inferred from the text as true
   - (c) can be inferred from the text as false
   - (d) cannot be inferred from the text and needs further research
4. Even if you eat junk food and never exercise, you can become a police officer.
   - (a) in the text
   - (b) can be inferred from the text as true
   - **(c) can be inferred from the text as false**
   - (d) cannot be inferred from the text and needs further research

PAGE 17

Police Officers Wanted

Read the newspaper advertisement. Then answer the questions.

WANTED: UNDERCOVER POLICE OFFICER

The Yountville Police Department is seeking undercover police officers to help monitor suspicious behavior in stores and in the community. Complete the application form located on the police department's website, www.yountvillepolice.org. Include your experience in safety; why you want to be an undercover police officer; your current health; and your favorite hobbies.

Please submit applications no later than July 7 to: Inspector Olson, Yountville Police Department.

1. What is the author's purpose for writing this advertisement?
   to inform the readers about a job opening
2. What does the right person for the job need to have or do?
   experience in safety and good health
3. What is the deadline for applying for the job?
   July 7
4. Who will be in charge of choosing the new undercover police officer?
   Inspector Olson
5. Which parts of the job description will probably make the biggest difference in whether or not a person can get this job?
   experience in safety and current health
6. Why do you think the police department wanted to know about applicants' hobbies?
   To see if the applicant enjoys things related to being a police officer.

PAGE 18

Honey

Read the passage. Then answer the questions.

Do you know which is the only insect that produces food eaten by humans? That's right! It's the honeybee. Honey is the only food that includes all of the substances necessary to live, including vitamins, minerals, and water. Did you know that honey comes in different shades and flavors? Darker honeys have more nutrients than lighter ones. There are over 300 unique flavors of honey in the United States, including maple, raspberry, and blackberry. The most common honey found in stores is called clover honey. In addition to being used with food, honey can also be used for medicinal purposes. Honey can help people suffering from allergies, heal cuts, and soothe a sore throat. The next time you see honey, take a closer look!

1. Based on the context clues, what are the nutrients found in honey?
   - (a) flavors
   - **(b) vitamins, minerals, and water**
   - (c) darker and lighter
   - (d) maple, raspberry, and blackberry
2. Based on the context clues, what does it mean to "use honey for its medicinal purposes"?
   - (a) how it makes food taste better
   - (b) how honey makes medicine
   - **(c) how honey can help people in ways similar to medicine**
   - (d) how honey can be sold to buy medicine
3. If you see two bottles of honey, one with darker honey and one lighter in color, what will you know?
   - (a) the darker honey is rotten
   - (b) the darker honey is hotter
   - (c) the lighter honey is not as heavy
   - **(d) the darker honey has more vitamins and minerals**
4. Write a fact about honey.
   Answers will vary.

PAGE 19

The BeeKeeper's Day

Read the To-Do List and Daily Log. Then answer the questions.

To-Do List for Today:
- Check the hives for insects, birds, and other intruders.
- Watch spy cam for skunk visit last night.
- Collect honey from the hives.

Daily Log
- 1:00 Speak at the Beekeepers Association Lunch about bee behavior when visited at night by skunks. Warn them of signs such as aggressive behavior the next day.
- 2:30 Check the bee swarms at Zydet Farm.
- 4:00 Make honey ice cream for the birthday party.
- 5:00 Bee Club meeting. Discuss how to keep intruders out of the hives.
- 6:30 Beatrice's birthday party.

1. What dessert will be served at Beatrice's birthday party?
   honey ice cream
2. Using context clues, do you think that insects and birds are good or bad for a beehive? Why or why not?
   They are bad. They are described as intruders. Intruders come without being invited.
3. Using context clues, do you think that skunks are good or bad for a beehive? Why or why not?
   Bees can be aggressive after a skunk visits a hive.
4. Use a dictionary to find the meaning of aggressive. What would aggressive behavior in bees most likely include?
   Aggressive behavior in bees might include flying out quickly at a beekeeper or stinging the keeper.

PAGE 21

Welcome to My Backyard

Use the passage on page 20 to write the missing cause or effect.

1. red flowers → attract hummingbirds
2. Buddleia or lavender → attract bees
3. yarrow → attracts ladybugs
4. Buddleia attracts → butterflies and bees
5. yarrow leaves → tea for stomachache
6. lavender → moth, flea
7. What is the common name for *Buddleia*?
   butterfly bush
8. What saying means *to invite someone or something in*?
   Lay out the welcome mat.
9. What does attract mean?
   To draw or invite in.

PAGE 23

Stay Away!

Use the passage on page 22 to answer the questions.

1. Problems: rabbits, squirrels, or dogs digging
   Solution: chili, or cayenne pepper
2. Problem: bugs
   Solution: planting basil
3. Problem: bugs
   Solution: planting rosemary
4. Problem: moles, mice, or aphids
   Solution: planting garlic
5. What are pests?
   unwanted creatures that ruin crops
6. Based on the passage on page 22 and what you know, what does the term *a natural repellant* mean?
   something that keeps pests away without the use of chemicals
7. How can someone keep pests out of a garden?
   plant certain plants in and around the garden

PAGE 24

Penguins

Read the passage. Then answer the questions on page 25.

All penguins in the wild live in the southern hemisphere, but they don't all live in Antarctica. Contrary to what is shown in most popular books and movies, all penguins do not live in the snow. In fact, one type of penguin, the Galapagos penguin, lives off the west coast of South America on the equator!

All penguins do live near water, because they spend most of their time in the ocean. Because their legs are so far back on their bodies, it is hard for them to walk on land. Instead, they prefer to slide on their bellies across the ground or swim with their webbed feet. They may not be able to fly in the air, but their powerful flippers are used like boat oars to help them "fly" through the water. Their feet and tails help them steer. The body of a penguin is streamlined, meaning that it allows for smooth movement through water. Whether in the icy lands of Antarctica or the warm islands near the equator, penguins are unique birds that enjoy living in groups called colonies.

PAGE 25

Penguins

Use the passage on page 24 to answer the questions.

1. Based on the context clues, what is the climate like near the equator?
   - (a) icy
   - (b) mild
   - **(c) warm**
2. Based on the context clues, what would something that is *streamlined* do?
   - (a) be as bumpy as a stream
   - (b) create layers of water
   - (c) make it harder to move through water
   - **(d) make it easier to move through water**
3. What does it mean when it says they "fly" through the water?
   - (a) They use their wings to fly through water.
   - (b) They fly in and out of the water.
   - **(c) They move quickly.**
4. Go back to the reading passage on page 24 and underline two words that would likely be in boldface print in a nonfiction book about penguins. Then use context clues to write the definition of each word on the lines below.
   1. streamlined - allows for smooth movement through the water.
   2. colonies - a group of penguins that live together.

PAGE 27

Pierre the Penguin

Use the passage on page 26 to answer the questions.

1. What is the author's purpose?
   - (a) entertain
   - (b) persuade
   - **(c) inform**
2. What is the theme of the story?
   - (a) penguins can swim
   - (b) penguins are special
   - **(c) penguins need feathers**
3. What was the first problem that resulted from Pierre's feathers falling out?
   Pierre was too cold to enter the water.
4. What was the second problem that resulted from Pierre's feathers falling out?
   The other penguins didn't recognize him and picked on him.
5. What was the solution to Pierre's problem?
   Pam had a wetsuit made so Pierre could stay warm in the water.
6. Based on information from the passage on page 26, did Pierre have to wear the wetsuit forever? Explain.
   No. The passage says his feathers grew back after six weeks.

PAGE 28

How Chocolate Is Made

Read the passage. Then write the numbers 1–7 on the lines to put the steps in order.

Do you like the smell or taste of chocolate? Where does chocolate come from? It all begins when farmers plant cacao trees. Hard fruit, called pods, grow on the trees. Within each pod are seeds called cacao beans. After many months, farm workers cut the pods off the trees. The cacao beans are taken out of the pods, left out to dry in the sun for many days, and are then put into large sacks. The dried cacao beans are taken to a chocolate factory, where they are made into chocolate. First, the beans must be cleaned. Next, they are roasted, which means they are cooked. This helps the shells come off more easily. After the shells are removed, the beans are smashed into a soft paste called cocoa butter. To make the chocolate, milk and sugar are added to the cocoa butter and are mixed together for several days. By mixing it, the chocolate becomes smooth and creamy. Like putting water into ice trays, the chocolate is poured into trays to cool and harden. Next, the chocolate is removed from the trays and machines wrap the chocolate to be sold in stores. Now you know where chocolate comes from.

4 cacao beans are cleaned and roasted
5 shells are removed and beans are smashed
3 cocoa beans dry in the sun
2 farmers cut the pods off the trees and remove cocoa beans
6 the milk, sugar, and cocoa butter are mixed and left to cool in trays
1 farmers plant cocoa trees
7 chocolate is removed from trays, wrapped, and sent to stores

PAGE 29

A Happy Accident

Read the passage. Then answer the questions.

One day in 1930, Ruth Wakefield was baking her favorite butter drop cookies when she realized that she was out of chocolate. She had accidentally forgotten to get the baker's chocolate she needed for her recipe. As a substitute, she decided to chop up a chocolate bar. Although she had hoped the chopped up chocolate would melt into her dough, it actually made little chocolate chips in her cookies. That accident led to the creation of the famous chocolate chip cookie!

At the time, Ruth Wakefield owned an inn called the Toll House Inn. She passed out her accidental cookie "invention" to the people who stayed at her inn. They loved them! A cookie company heard of her creation and named their now famous chocolate chips after her inn. Her recipe is on the back of each bag of Toll House chocolate chips found at the store today. From an accident while baking cookies, many people are happily eating chocolate chip cookies today.

1. What was the author's purpose?
   - (a) entertain
   - (b) persuade
   - **(c) inform**
2. Chocolate chip cookies were accidentally "invented" by Ruth Wakefied.
   - **(a) fact**
   - (b) opinion
3. Everyone loves chocolate chip cookies.
   - (a) fact
   - **(b) opinion**
4. What was the effect of Ruth Wakefield not having the chocolate she needed to make her cookies?
   She chopped up a chocolate bar and added it to the dough.
5. Why do you think the recipe on the back of the chocolate chips is called the "Toll House Chocolate Chip Cookies"?
   At the time she "invented" chocolate chip cookies, she owned the Toll House Inn.

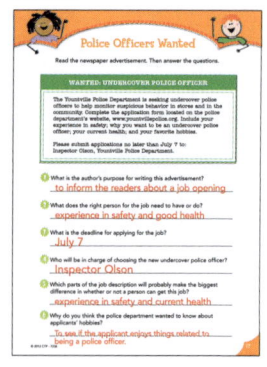

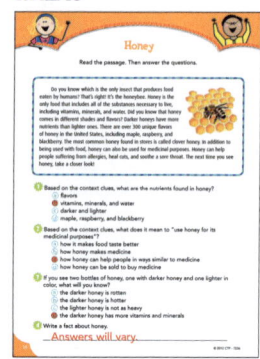

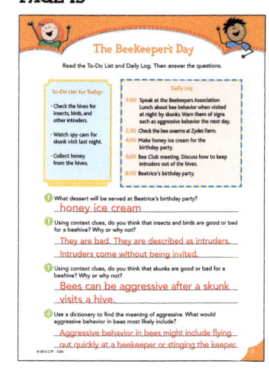

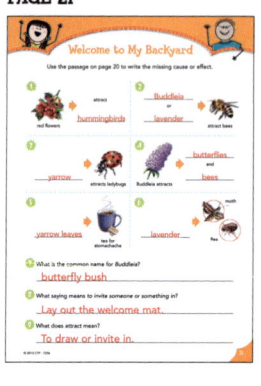

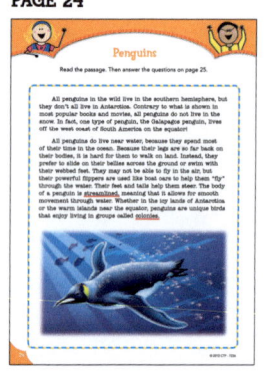

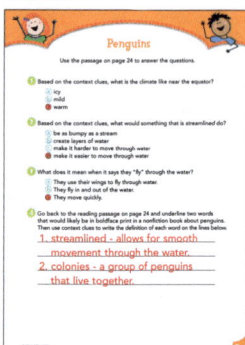

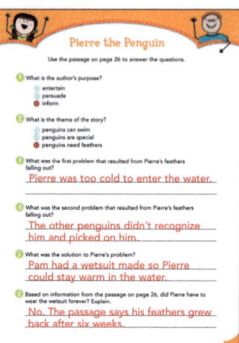

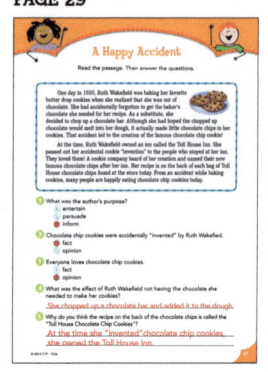

PAGE 30

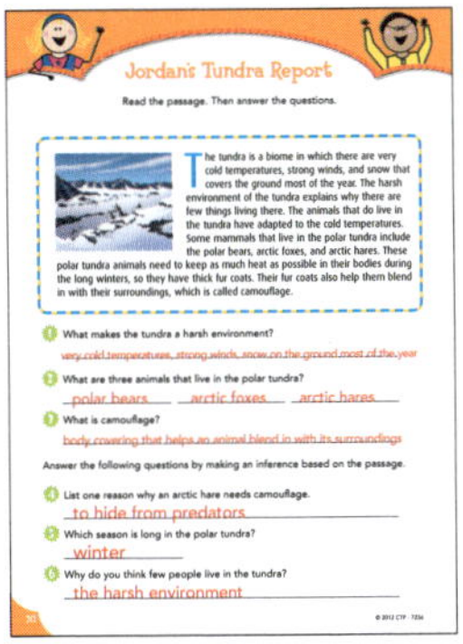

PAGE 31

PAGE 32

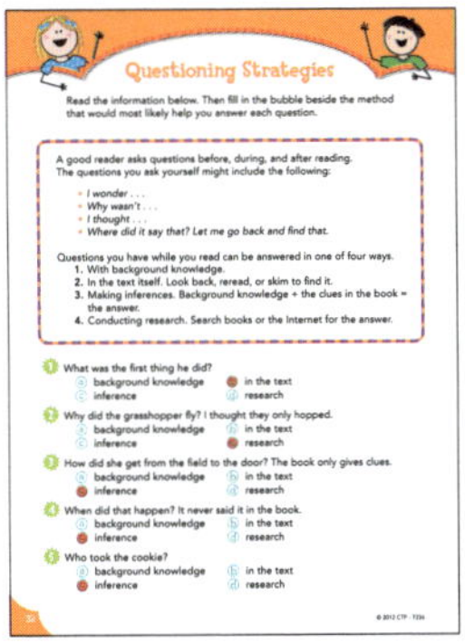

PAGE 33

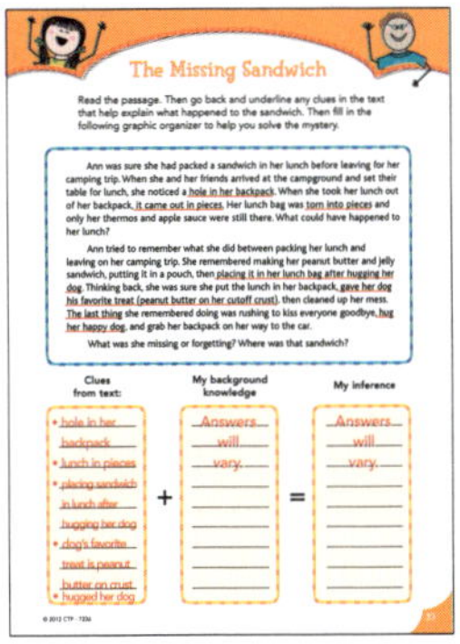

PAGE 34

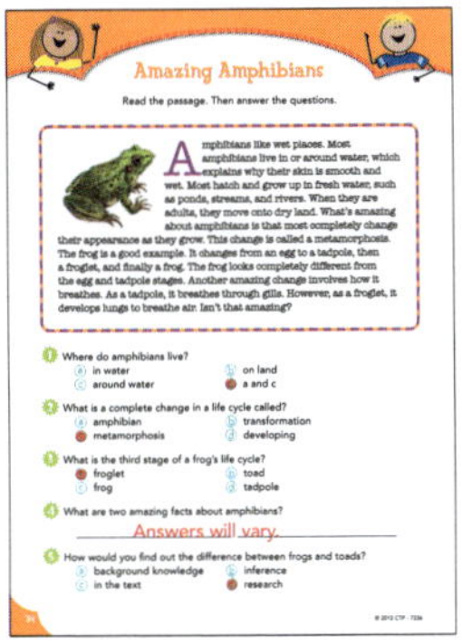

PAGE 35

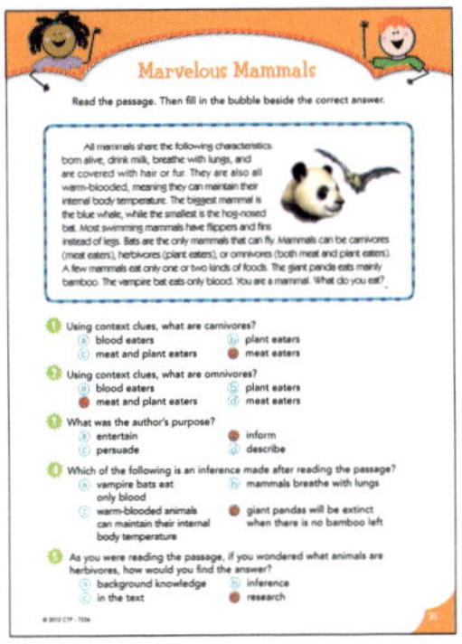

PAGE 36

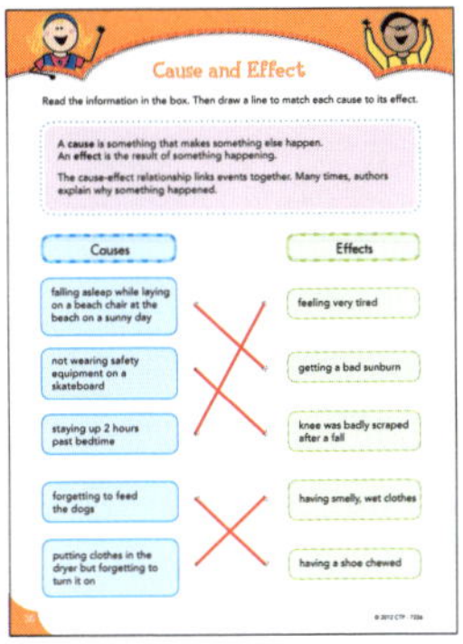

PAGE 37

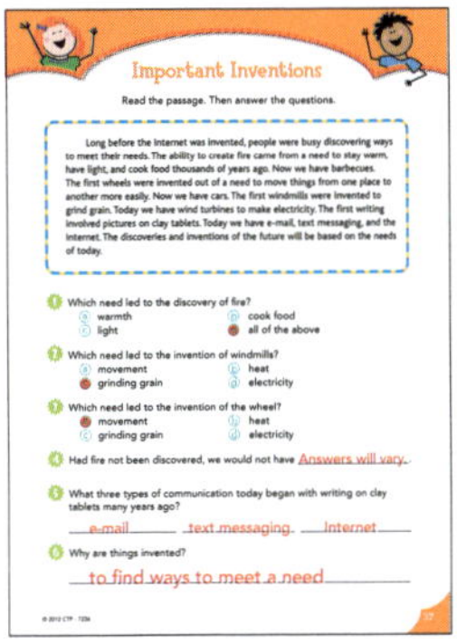

PAGE 38

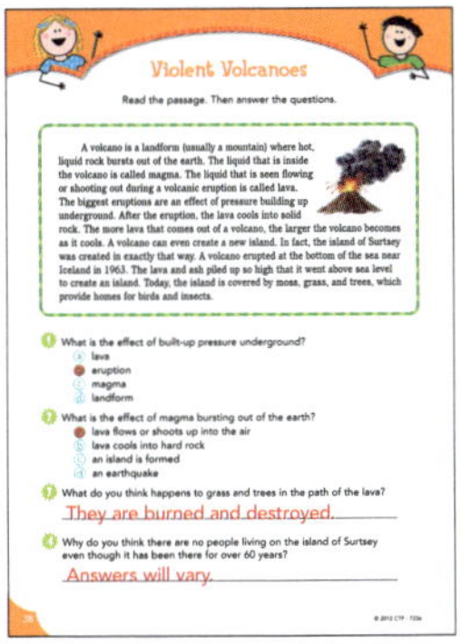

PAGE 39

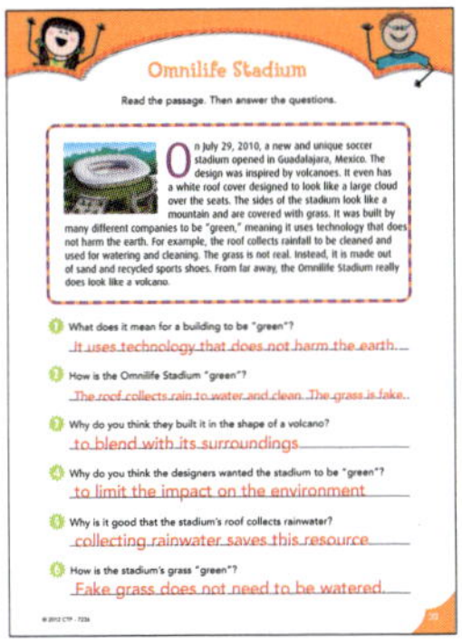

PAGE 40

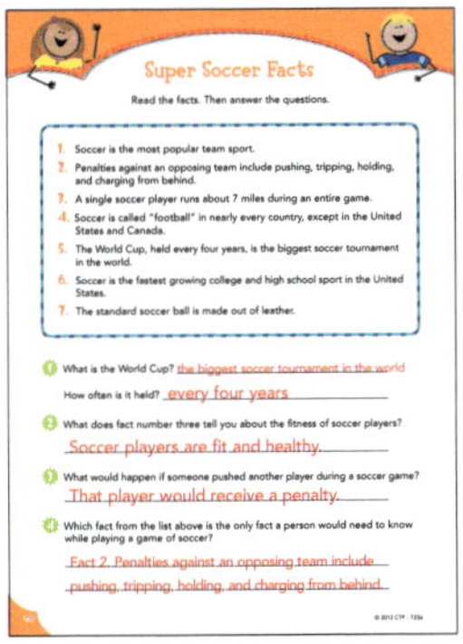

PAGE 41

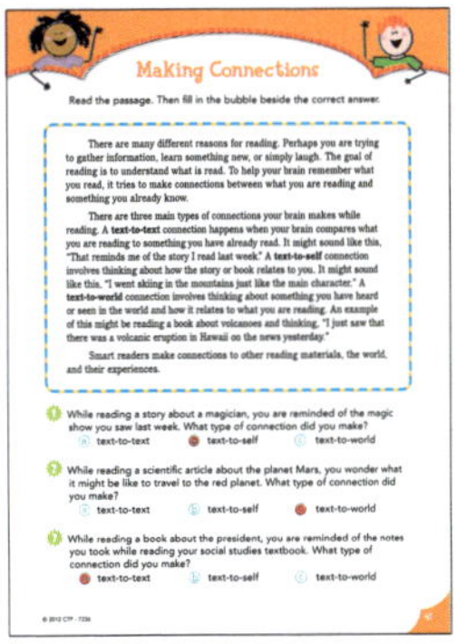

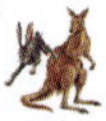

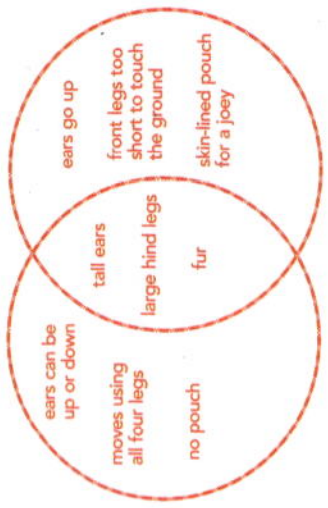

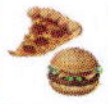

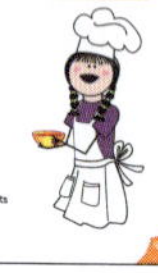

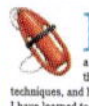

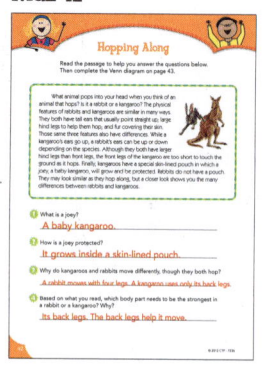

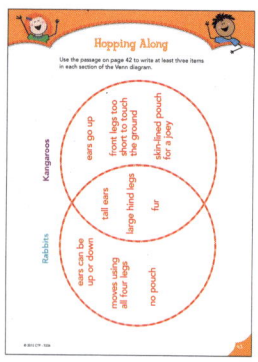

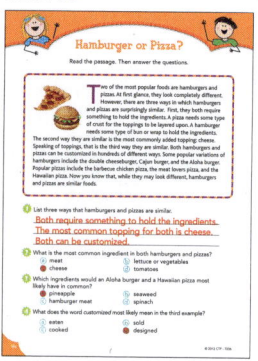

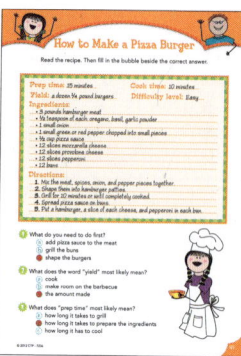

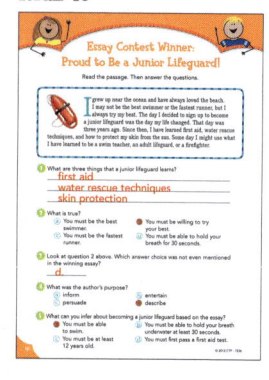

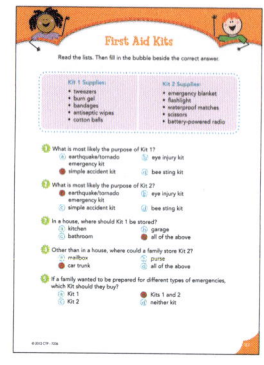

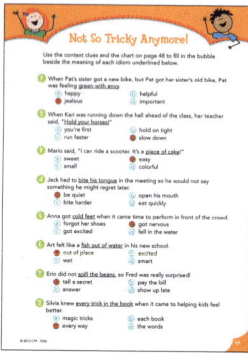

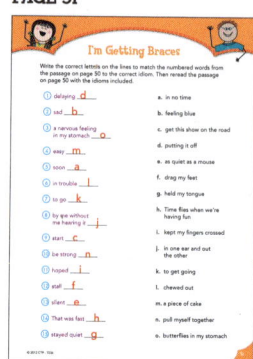

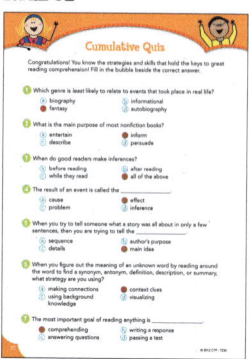